001   The war on
        terrorism

The War on
TERRORISM

O P P O S I N G   V I E W P O I N T S ®

Karen F. Balkin, *Book Editor*

Bruce Glassman, *Vice President*
Bonnie Szumski, *Publisher*
Helen Cothran, *Managing Editor*

OPPOSING
VIEWPOINTS®
SERIES

GREENHAVEN PRESS
An imprint of Thomson Gale, a part of The Thomson Corporation

THOMSON

GALE

Detroit • New York • San Francisco • San Diego • New Haven, Conn.
Waterville, Maine • London • Munich

THOMSON

✳

™

GALE

LIBRARY OF CONGRESS CATALOGING-IN-PUBLICATION DATA

The war on terrorism : opposing viewpoints / Karen F. Balkin, book editor.
 p. cm. — (Opposing viewpoints series)
 Includes bibliographical references and index.
 ISBN 0-7377-2336-X (lib. : alk. paper) — ISBN 0-7377-2337-8 (pbk. : alk. paper)
  1. War on terrorism, 2001– . 2. Terrorism—United States—Prevention.
 3. United States—Foreign relations—2001– . I. Balkin, Karen F., 1949– . II. Series
 HV6432.W373 2005
 973.931—dc22   2004047442

Printed in the United States of America

"Congress shall make no law...abridging the freedom of speech, or of the press."

First Amendment to the U.S. Constitution

The basic foundation of our democracy is the First Amendment guarantee of freedom of expression. The Opposing Viewpoints Series is dedicated to the concept of this basic freedom and the idea that it is more important to practice it than to enshrine it.

Contents

Chapter 3: Will the Domestic Antiterrorism Measures Make Americans Safer?

Chapter 4: How Is the U.S. War on Terrorism Affecting the World?

Why Consider Opposing Viewpoints?

"The only way in which a human being can make some approach to knowing the whole of a subject is by hearing what can be said about it by persons of every variety of opinion and studying all modes in which it can be looked at by every character of mind. No wise man ever acquired his wisdom in any mode but this."

John Stuart Mill

In our media-intensive culture it is not difficult to find differing opinions. Thousands of newspapers and magazines and dozens of radio and television talk shows resound with differing points of view. The difficulty lies in deciding which opinion to agree with and which "experts" seem the most credible. The more inundated we become with differing opinions and claims, the more essential it is to hone critical reading and thinking skills to evaluate these ideas. Opposing Viewpoints books address this problem directly by presenting stimulating debates that can be used to enhance and teach these skills. The varied opinions contained in each book examine many different aspects of a single issue. While examining these conveniently edited opposing views, readers can develop critical thinking skills such as the ability to compare and contrast authors' credibility, facts, argumentation styles, use of persuasive techniques, and other stylistic tools. In short, the Opposing Viewpoints Series is an ideal way to attain the higher-level thinking and reading skills so essential in a culture of diverse and contradictory opinions.

In addition to providing a tool for critical thinking, Opposing Viewpoints books challenge readers to question their own strongly held opinions and assumptions. Most people form their opinions on the basis of upbringing, peer pressure, and personal, cultural, or professional bias. By reading carefully balanced opposing views, readers must directly confront new ideas as well as the opinions of those with whom they disagree. This is not to simplistically argue that everyone who reads opposing views will—or should—change his or her opinion. Instead, the series enhances readers' understanding of their own views by encouraging confrontation with opposing ideas. Careful examination of others' views can lead to the readers' understanding of the logical inconsistencies in their own opinions, perspective on why they hold an opinion, and the consideration of the possibility that their opinion requires further evaluation.

Evaluating Other Opinions

To ensure that this type of examination occurs, Opposing Viewpoints books present all types of opinions. Prominent spokespeople on different sides of each issue as well as well-known professionals from many disciplines challenge the reader. An additional goal of the series is to provide a forum for other, less known, or even unpopular viewpoints. The opinion of an ordinary person who has had to make the decision to cut off life support from a terminally ill relative, for example, may be just as valuable and provide just as much insight as a medical ethicist's professional opinion. The editors have two additional purposes in including these less known views. One, the editors encourage readers to respect others' opinions—even when not enhanced by professional credibility. It is only by reading or listening to and objectively evaluating others' ideas that one can determine whether they are worthy of consideration. Two, the inclusion of such viewpoints encourages the important critical thinking skill of objectively evaluating an author's credentials and bias. This evaluation will illuminate an author's reasons for taking a particular stance on an issue and will aid in readers' evaluation of the author's ideas.

It is our hope that these books will give readers a deeper understanding of the issues debated and an appreciation of the complexity of even seemingly simple issues when good and honest people disagree. This awareness is particularly important in a democratic society such as ours in which people enter into public debate to determine the common good. Those with whom one disagrees should not be regarded as enemies but rather as people whose views deserve careful examination and may shed light on one's own.

Thomas Jefferson once said that "difference of opinion leads to inquiry, and inquiry to truth." Jefferson, a broadly educated man, argued that "if a nation expects to be ignorant and free . . . it expects what never was and never will be." As individuals and as a nation, it is imperative that we consider the opinions of others and examine them with skill and discernment. The Opposing Viewpoints Series is intended to help readers achieve this goal.

David L. Bender and Bruno Leone,
Founders

Greenhaven Press anthologies primarily consist of previously published material taken from a variety of sources, including periodicals, books, scholarly journals, newspapers, government documents, and position papers from private and public organizations. These original sources are often edited for length and to ensure their accessibility for a young adult audience. The anthology editors also change the original titles of these works in order to clearly present the main thesis of each viewpoint and to explicitly indicate the opinion presented in the viewpoint. These alterations are made in consideration of both the reading and comprehension levels of a young adult audience. Every effort is made to ensure that Greenhaven Press accurately reflects the original intent of the authors included in this anthology.

Introduction

"Biological terrorism provides paramilitary groups and terrorists a means to make their point and do it very dramatically."

—*Army Brigadier General John Doesberg*

The purpose of all forms of terrorism—including bioterrorism—is to create fear and intimidate individuals, governments, or societies into capitulating to terrorists' religious, political, or ideological demands. The terrorists' goal is not to cause massive death or destruction but to inspire panic within a population. Thus, bioterrorism—defined by scientists as the unlawful use, or threatened use, of microorganisms or toxins derived from microorganisms to produce illness or disease in humans, animals, or plants—has become an important issue in the U.S. war on terrorism.

While modern technology has improved the production and distribution of biological weapons, their use is not new. Historical accounts of the siege of Kaffa (a port on the Crimean Peninsula in the Black Sea) in 1346 include a report of an outbreak of plague caused when the attacking Tatars catapulted infected corpses into the city. During the American Revolution, the British tried to infect the Continental army with smallpox and were successful on several occasions. The use by the British and Americans of smallpox-infected blankets to cause disease among Native American tribes is also well documented. German scientists and military officials targeted livestock during World War I, trying to spread disease among cattle, horses, sheep, and mules shipped to the Allies by neutral countries. The Germans and Japanese used prisoners to experiment with lethal viruses during World War II.

In 1942 the United States began an offensive biological weapons program that intensified and reached its peak during the Cold War. Then-president Richard Nixon ended the program in 1969 and ordered all existing stocks of biological weapons destroyed. The Soviets, however, continued to produce and stockpile lethal biological agents through the 1980s.

Many U.S. scientists and government officials claim that when the Cold War ended and the Soviets finally stopped their biological weapons research, scientists from that country used their knowledge and skills to help other nations develop the biological agents that have become the basis for twenty-first-century bioterrorism.

Most recently, Iraq developed a significant biological weapons arsenal between 1985 and 1991, according to weapons experts. While these agents were not used in the Persian Gulf War, some military authorities argue that they were employed during the Iran-Iraq War. Trace amounts of anthrax and mycotoxins (toxic substances produced by fungi and molds) were found in Iranian casualties during that war. After the Gulf War, Iraq claimed to have destroyed all its biological weapons. The United Nations Special Commission tried to conduct inspections in accordance with the terms that ended the Gulf War, but it was hampered by the lack of Iraqi cooperation and thus could not verify these claims. When coalition forces invaded Iraq in 2003 to rid the nation of weapons of mass destruction, they did not find evidence of biological weapons. However, facilities that produce biological weapons are often difficult to detect because the equipment used is designed for dual purposes—the production of biological agents and the manufacture of other, more benign products. The worldwide concern is that the biological weapons Iraq once possessed were not destroyed but have found their way into the hands of international terrorists. In any event, even if terrorists were unable to buy biological agents from nations such as Iraq, any terrorist organization with access to the Internet and the moderately sophisticated technology can produce biological weapons. Indeed, a bioterrorist attack has had experts worried since before the September 11, 2001, terrorist attack on the United States. As former defense secretary William Cohen said, "This scenario of a nuclear, biological or chemical weapon in the hands of a terrorist cell or rogue nation is not only plausible, it's really quite real."

A bioterrorist attack could be catastrophic. According to D.A. Henderson, former director of the World Health Organization's global smallpox eradication project, a biological agent such as smallpox could be released undetected into a crowded area. Days would pass before victims would begin reporting symptoms and requesting treatment. By then the disease would have spread secondarily to many other people, and a full-scale epidemic would ensue. Further, diagnosing diseases not commonly seen would require time and specialized laboratory facilities. R.J. Bellamy and A.R. Freedman of the Department of Infectious Diseases at the University Hospital of Wales in England maintain that "the majority of physicians practicing today have never seen cases of smallpox, pneumonic plague, typhoidal tularaemia, pulmonary anthrax nor many other diseases that could result from a bioterrorist attack." Indeed, many doctors and researchers argue that the United States is not prepared for a bioterrorist attack. Bruce Clements, associate director of St. Louis University's Center for the Study of Bioterrorism and Emerging Infections warns that "we are woefully unprepared." In addition to the concern over shortages, some doctors and public health officials claim that plans are not in place in most cities for the efficient distribution of the stockpiles of antibiotics and equipment that do exist.

Authors in *Opposing Viewpoints: The War on Terrorism* debate the issues that surround America's war on terrorism in the following chapters: Is the War on Terrorism Justified? Is the Domestic War on Terrorism a Threat to Civil Liberties? Will the Domestic Antiterrorism Measures Make Americans Safer? How Is the U.S. War on Terrorism Affecting the World? Not only does the United States face the enormous task of reducing the threats posed by terrorists, including their use of biological weapons, U.S. officials are also subject to criticisms, as the wide range of views in this volume demonstrate.

CHAPTER 1

Is the War on Terrorism Justified?

Chapter Preface

One of the most controversial aspects of the U.S. war on terrorism is the preemptive war against Iraq, begun on March 19, 2003. A preemptive war is one in which one country attacks another believed to be an imminent threat. While domestic measures such as heightened security efforts seem clearly necessary to win the war on terrorism, the justification for preemptive war is less clear and therefore open to greater debate. President George W. Bush argued that the attack on Baghdad was legally and morally justified based on the terrorist threat posed by Iraq. Many experts agree with Bush, contending that international law and the United Nations Charter confirm a country's right to self-defense. That right includes the ancient principle of "anticipatory self-defense," which allows one country to attack another when faced with an imminent threat to its national security. However, many domestic and international legal scholars and political experts insist that Iraq presented no immediate terrorist threat to the United States, and thus a preemptive attack on that country was an unprovoked act of aggression

The Bush administration maintains that the strategy of deterrence—weapons inspections and no-fly zones—and the embargos used against Iraq for the past two decades did not reduce the Iraqi threat to the United States or the world. According to Kenneth Pollack, senior fellow at the Brookings Institution, "There is a very sound, strategic rationale for going to war with Iraq. It is derived from a threat that Saddam Hussein poses to the region, to the world, to the United States from his determination to acquire nuclear weapons, his determination to turn Iraq into a new superpower, to dominate, if not control the Persian Gulf and its vital oil resources." Further, proponents of preemptive war claim that military victory in Iraq will help reduce terrorism conducted by organizations such as al Qaeda, Hezbollah, and Islamic Jihad, which operate with the support of many Middle Eastern nations, including Iraq.

Those who opposed the preemptive war against Iraq, however, claim that no factual link has ever been proven between Iraq and al Qaeda or other Middle Eastern terrorist groups.

Moreover, they assert that Iraq's secular regime under Saddam Hussein was openly antagonistic to fundamentalist Islamic organizations. Further, the Bush administration's doctrine of preemptive war reversed the U.S. no-strike-first policy followed since the end of World War II, setting a dangerous precedent for other countries, many war critics contend. The UN's traditional opposition to preemptive war is based on a similar philosophy expressed in its charter—that a war in self-defense can only be claimed when a country has been attacked, not when its leaders believe that it might be attacked.

Whether the preemptive war against Iraq can be considered legitimate is just one of the controversies surrounding the war on terrorism. Authors in the following chapter examine other justifications for the war.

"The proper response [to acts of terrorism], as the public now understands, is a war in self-defense."

End States Who Sponsor Terrorism

Dr. Leonard Peikoff

The United States has the duty to defend itself against terrorists by going to war against the regimes that make terrorism possible. The war should be fought with the most effective weapons despite the collateral damage to foreign civilians. Dr. Leonard Peikoff is the founder of the Ayn Rand Institute in Irvine, California.

As you read, consider the following questions:
1. Why was the United States silent when Iran nationalized its oil industry in 1951?
2. Which country is the most active state sponsor of terrorism?
3. Which is the greatest obstacle to a U.S. victory over terrorism?

Fifty years of increasing American appeasement in the Mideast have led to fifty years of increasing contempt in the Muslim world for the U.S. The climax was September 11, 2001 [when Middle Eastern terrorists attacked the United States].

Fifty years ago, [President Harry S.] Truman and [President Dwight D.] Eisenhower surrendered the West's property rights in oil, although that oil rightfully belonged to those in the West whose science, technology, and capital made its discovery and use possible. The first country to nationalize Western oil, in 1951, was Iran. The rest, observing our frightened silence, hurried to grab their piece of the newly available loot.

The cause of the U.S. silence was not practical, but philosophical. The Mideast's dictators were denouncing wealthy egotistical capitalism. They were crying that their poor needed our sacrifice; that oil, like all property, is owned collectively, by virtue of birth; and that they knew their viewpoint was true by means of otherworldly emotion. Our Presidents had no answer. Implicitly, they were ashamed of the Declaration of Independence. They did not dare to answer that Americans, properly, were motivated by the selfish desire to achieve personal happiness in a rich, secular, individualist society.

The Muslim countries embodied in an extreme form every idea—selfless duty, anti-materialism, faith or feeling above science, the supremacy of the group—which our universities, our churches, and our own political Establishment had long been upholding as virtue. When two groups, our leadership and theirs, accept the same basic ideas, the most consistent side wins.

After property came liberty. "The Muslim fundamentalist movement," writes Yale historian Lamin Sanneh, "began in 1979 with the Iranian [theocratic] revolution. . . ." During his first year as its leader, Ayatollah Khomeini, urging a Jihad against "the Great Satan," kidnapped 52 U.S. diplomatic personnel and held them hostage; [President Jimmy] Carter's reaction was fumbling paralysis. About a decade later, Iran topped this evil. Khomeini issued his infamous Fatwa aimed at censoring, even outside his borders, any ideas uncongenial to Muslim sensibility. This was the meaning of his threat to kill British author [Salman] Rushdie and to destroy his American publisher; their crime was the exercise of their right to express an unpopular intellectual viewpoint. The Fatwa was Iran's attempt, reaffirmed after Khomeini's death, to stifle, anywhere in the world, the very process of thought. [President George] Bush Sr. looked the other way.

Iran Is the Most Active Sponsor of Terror

After liberty came American life itself. The first killers were the Palestinian hijackers of the late 1960s. But the killing spree which has now shattered our soaring landmarks, our daily routine, and our souls, began in earnest only after the license granted by Carter and Bush Sr.

Many nations work to fill our body bags. But Iran, according to a State Department report of 1999, is "the most active state sponsor of terrorism," training and arming groups from all over the Mideast, including Islamic Jihad, Hamas, and Hezbollah. Nor is Iran's government now "moderating." Five months ago [May 2001], the world's leading terrorist groups resolved to unite in a holy war against the U.S., which they called "a second Israel"; their meeting was held in Teheran.

What has been the U.S. response to the above? In 1996, nineteen U.S. soldiers were killed in their barracks in Saudi Arabia. According to a front-page story in *The New York Times* "Evidence suggesting that Iran sponsored the attack has further complicated the investigation, because the United States and Saudi Arabia have recently sought to improve relations with a new, relatively moderate Government in Teheran." In other words, [President Bill] Clinton evaded Iran's role because he wanted what he called "a genuine reconciliation." In public, of course, he continued to vow that he would find and punish the guilty. This inaction of Clinton's is comparable to his action after [Osama] bin Laden's attack on U.S. embassies in East Africa; his action was the gingerly bombing of two meaningless targets.

Conservatives are equally responsible for today's crisis, as [President Ronald] Reagan's record attests. Reagan not only failed to retaliate after 241 U.S. marines in Lebanon were slaughtered; he did worse. Holding that Islamic guerrillas were our ideological allies because of their fight against the atheistic Soviets, he methodically poured money and expertise into Afghanistan. This put the U.S. wholesale into the business of creating terrorists. Most of them regarded fighting the Soviets as only the beginning; our turn soon came.

For over a decade, there was another guarantee of American impotence: the notion that a terrorist is alone responsible for his actions, and that each, therefore, must be tried as an individual before a court of law. This viewpoint, thankfully, is fading; most people now understand that terrorists exist only through the sanction and support of a government.

Terrorism Is an Act of War

We need not prove the identity of any of these creatures, because terrorism is not an issue of personalities. It cannot be stopped by destroying bin Laden and [his] al-Qaeda army, or even by destroying the destroyers everywhere. If that is all we do, a new army of militants will soon rise up to replace the old one.

The behavior of such militants is that of the regimes which make them possible. Their atrocities are not crimes, but acts of war. The proper response, as the public now understands, is a war in self-defense. In the excellent words of Paul Wolfowitz, deputy secretary of defense, we must "end states who sponsor terrorism."

A proper war in self-defense is one fought without self-crippling restrictions placed on our commanders in the field. It must be fought with the most effective weapons we possess (. . . [Secretary of Defense Donald H.] Rumsfeld refused, correctly, to rule out nuclear weapons). And it must be fought in a manner that secures victory as quickly as possible and with the fewest U.S. casualties, regardless of the countless innocents caught in the line of fire. These innocents suffer and die because of the action of their own government in sponsoring the initiation of force against America. Their fate, therefore, is their government's moral responsibility. There is no way for our bullets to be aimed only at evil men.

The public understandably demands retaliation against Afghanistan [which harbored al-Qaeda terrorists]. But in the wider context Afghanistan is insignificant. It is too devastated even to breed many fanatics. Since it is no more these days than a place to hide, its elimination would do little to end terrorism.

Terrorism is a specific disease, which can be treated only by a specific antidote. The nature of the disease (though not of its antidote) has been suggested by Serge Schmemann. Our struggle now, he writes, is "not a struggle against a conventional guerrilla force, whose yearning for a national homeland or the satisfaction of some grievance could be satisfied or denied. The terrorists [on September 11] . . . issued no demands, no ultimatums. They did it solely out of grievance and hatred—hatred for the values cherished in the West as freedom, tolerance, prosperity, religious pluralism and universal suffrage, but abhorred by religious fundamentalists (and not only Muslim fundamentalists) as licentiousness, corruption, greed and apostasy."

The Struggle Against Terrorism Is a Struggle of Ideas

Every word of this is true. The obvious implication is that the struggle against terrorism is not a struggle over Palestine. It is a clash of cultures, and thus a struggle of ideas, which can be dealt with, ultimately, only by intellectual means. But this fact does not depreciate the crucial role of our armed forces. On the contrary, it increases their effectiveness, by pointing them to the right target.

Most of the Mideast is ruled by thugs who would be paralyzed by an American victory over any of their neighbors. Iran, by contrast, is the only major country there ruled by zealots dedicated not to material gain (such as more wealth or territory), but to the triumph by any means, however violent, of the Muslim fundamentalist movement they brought to life. That is why Iran manufactures the most terrorists.

If one were under a Nazi aerial bombardment, it would be senseless to restrict oneself to combatting Nazi satellites while ignoring Germany and the ideological plague it was working to spread. What Germany was to Nazism in the 1940s, Iran is to terrorism today. Whatever else it does, therefore, the U.S. can put an end to the Jihad-mongers only by taking out Iran.

Eliminating Iran's terrorist sanctuaries and military capability is not enough. We must do the equivalent of de-Nazifying the country, by expelling every official and bringing down every branch of its government. This goal cannot be achieved painlessly, by weaponry alone. It requires invasion by ground troops, who will be at serious risk, and perhaps a period of occupation. But nothing less will "end the state" that most cries out to be ended.

The greatest obstacle to U.S. victory is not Iran and its allies, but our own intellectuals. Even now, they are advocating the same ideas that caused our historical paralysis. They are asking a reeling nation to show neighbor-love by shunning "vengeance." The multiculturalists—rejecting the concept of objectivity—are urging us to "understand" the Arabs and avoid "racism" (i.e., any condemnation of any group's culture). The friends of "peace" are reminding us, ever more loudly, to "remember Hiroshima" and beware the sin of pride.

End States That Sponsor Terrorism

These are the kinds of voices being heard in the universities, the churches, and the media as the country recovers from its first shock, and the professoriate et al. feel emboldened to resume business as usual. These voices are a siren song luring us to untroubled sleep while the fanatics proceed to gut America.

Tragically, Mr. [George W.] Bush is attempting a compromise between the people's demand for a decisive war and the intellectuals' demand for appeasement.

It is likely that the Bush administration will soon launch an attack on bin Laden's organization in Afghanistan and possibly even attack the Taliban. Despite this, however, every sign indicates that Mr. Bush will repeat the mistakes made by his father in Iraq. As of October 1, the Taliban leadership appears not to be a target. Even worse, the administration refuses to target Iran, or any of the other countries identified by the State Department as terrorist regimes. On the contrary, [Secretary of State Colin] Powell is seeking to add to the current coalition these very states—which is the equivalent of going into partnership with the Soviet Union in order to fight Communism (under the pretext, say, of proving that we are not anti-Russian). By seeking such a coalition, our President is asserting that he needs the support of terrorist nations in order to fight them. He is stating publicly that the world's only superpower does not have enough self-confidence or moral courage to act unilaterally in its own defense.

For some days now, Mr. Bush has been downplaying the role of our military, while praising the same policies (mainly negotiation and economic pressure) that have failed so spectacularly and for so long. Instead of attacking the roots of global terrorism, he seems to be settling for a "guerrilla war" against al-Qaeda, and a policy of unseating the Taliban passively, by aiding a motley coalition of native tribes. Our battle, he stresses, will be a "lengthy" one. Later, in fall 2001, he did remove the Taliban, at least for a while.

Mr. Bush's compromise will leave the primary creators of terrorism whole—and unafraid. His approach might satisfy our short-term desire for retribution, but it will guarantee catastrophe in the long term.

As yet, however, no overall policy has been solidified; the administration still seems to be groping. And an angry public still expects our government not merely to hobble terrorism for a while, but to eradicate it. The only hope left is that Mr. Bush will listen to the public, not to the professors and their progeny.

The Survival of America Is at Stake

When should we act, if not now? If our appeasement has led to an escalation of disasters in the past, can it do otherwise in the future? Do we wait until our enemies master nuclear, chemical, and biological warfare?

The survival of America is at stake. The risk of a U.S. overreaction, therefore, is negligible. The only risk is underreaction.

Mr. Bush must reverse course. He must send our missiles and troops, in force, where they belong. And he must justify this action by declaring with righteous conviction that we have discarded the clichés of our paper-tiger past and that the U.S. now places America first.

There is still time to demonstrate that we take the war against terrorism seriously—as a sacred obligation to our

Founding Fathers, to every victim of the men who hate this country, and to ourselves. There is still time to make the world understand that we will take up arms, anywhere and on principle, to secure an American's right to life, liberty, and the pursuit of happiness on earth.

The choice today is mass death in the United States or mass death in the terrorist nations. Our Commander-In-Chief must decide whether it is his duty to save Americans or the governments who conspire to kill them.

"The 'war on terror' has produced only more war and more terror."

War Exacerbates Terrorism

Independent/UK

The world was not forever changed by the September 11, 2001, terrorist attacks on the United States. What changed, editors of the British *Independent/UK* argue in the following viewpoint, was America's mood. They contend that as U.S. optimism and confidence turned to fear, and the need for security replaced the desire for freedom, President George W. Bush responded by declaring a war on terror. The editors maintain that the war on terror is unsuccessful and has only exacerbated war and terror in the world. The *Independent/UK* is an online and print publication, with editions throughout the United Kingdom.

As you read, consider the following questions:

1. According to the editors of the *Independent/UK*, what has happened to the gap between rich and poor in the world since the September 11, 2001, terrorist attacks on the United States?
2. What do the editors argue is the most dangerous and futile conclusion drawn from the September 11, 2001, terrorist attacks?
3. To what do the authors attribute the failures of the war on terror?

Two years is but the blinking of an eye in world history, especially in this new and fast-moving century. The events of two years ago today [September 11, 2001], however, now seem strangely distant, reminders of a past, perhaps more innocent, age.

The images of hijacked planes smashing into the twin towers of the World Trade Center on a crystalline day in New York still have the power to shock. It is still hard to see a plane flying above skyscrapers anywhere without recalling the date, 11 September [2001] when we first understood that such spectacular acts of destruction were possible. The stories of heroism and survival retain their inspirational power, as does the determination of New Yorkers to stand by their city.

Many of the assumptions and judgments made in the aftermath of what will always be known simply as 11 September, however, now seem sorely misplaced, even wrong.

Lofty Conclusions

Contrary to what many believed, the world was not changed forever by these co-ordinated attacks on American power. There were terrorist atrocities before and since, though none so daring in conception and execution, or as costly in lives, as those of two years ago. What was changed was the mood of America. Optimism and confidence gave way to defensiveness and fear. Security became the watchword for all. A weak and untested President found himself immeasurably strengthened. Americans rallied to the banner of patriotism he held aloft; the world's sympathy and support flooded in.

Most of the loftier, more universal conclusions drawn from 11 September, however, have not been justified. At worst, they have proved dangerously counterproductive. The hopes expressed, among others, by [British prime minister] Tony Blair for a more united world, in which the gap between rich and poor could be narrowed to mutual benefit, have not been fulfilled. If anything, the divisions have widened. The pictures of those hijacked planes and the wreckage at Ground Zero have not been heeded as a warning of anything except the vulnerability of the Western world. They have done nothing to raise aid budgets or divert investment to the developing world. They have done noth-

Auth. © 1986 by *The Philadelphia Inquirer*. Reproduced by permission of Universal Press Syndicate.

ing to enhance understanding of the Islamic world. In the United States, at least, almost the reverse has been true.

Civil liberties have been circumscribed as at no time since the McCarthyite witch-hunts of the Cold War [when people perceived to be Communists were targeted]. The supposed requirements of Homeland Security take precedence over everything else. Other countries, Britain included, have quietly followed Washington's lead. But neither individual countries, nor the world, have become significantly safer as a result. So long as there are disaffected groups, with the means and imagination to attack, acts of terrorism are going to be a fact of life that governments must steel their countries against, while recognizing—as the Israeli security fence has shown—that total prevention is an impossibility.

The "War on Terror"

Of all the conclusions drawn from 11 September, however, the "war on terror" declared by President [George W.] Bush in its wake has been at once the most dangerous and the most futile. Few would dispute the designation of those attacks as terrorist acts. Whether, as Mr Bush and others determined at the time, they also constituted acts of war is a point that can be debated.

The attack on Afghanistan [in Fall 2001], launched as a massive reprisal for the attacks on New York and Washington, is defensible as an attempt to root out the bases of al-Qa'ida, the group held responsible for the 11 September attacks, as for other attacks on US interests elsewhere. President Bush prepared for the campaign cautiously and mustered a coalition. A new government was established under international auspices with international protection.

There is room for skepticism here; the dominance of the United States in the campaign and the fragility of the new government without US support, the re-encroachment of warlords and the return of the opium poppies all pose questions about how effective or worthwhile the military campaign was.

When it comes to Iraq [against which America went to war in 2003], there is no place for even that degree of skepticism: the result is clear. Here we have a war embarked upon unilaterally, on the basis of spurious intelligence, to change a regime for which there was no tenable replacement—except an inadequate army of occupation.

Unlit Beacons

This is where Mr Bush's "war on terror" has brought us. Two years on, its successes are minimal; its failings stand as monuments to US misconceptions about the world and the reach of state power. The chief villains identified by the US are all still at large. Afghanistan is far from pacified. The Taliban [regime in Afghanistan] are regrouping. Iraqis lack basic services and law and order—even though it is the duty of the occupation forces to provide them. The Middle East is in flames and the road-map [to peace between Israel and the Palestinians] is in shreds. The beacons of democracy that were going to shine from Baghdad remain unlit.

This may be a uniquely pessimistic moment—another blinking of an eye, that will soon yield a vision of something better. Mr Bush is returning to the UN. US public opinion may be shifting away from its fearfulness. But as the attack on the UN headquarters in Baghdad so graphically showed, the whole region is as much a magnet for unruly armed force as ever. The "war on terror" has produced only more war and more terror.

"*Today the war on terrorism and the struggle for oil have become one vast enterprise.*"

The War on Terrorism Is Really a Struggle for Oil

Michael T. Klare

Michael T. Klare argues in the following viewpoint that the U.S. war on terrorism has merged with the struggle for oil because many of the word's largest petroleum reserves are in unstable regions prone to strife and terrorism. He maintains that the war on terrorism provides a convenient rationale for military involvement in oil-rich areas. America should wean itself off of foreign oil to avoid continuous involvement in foreign conflicts. Michael T. Klare is a professor of peace and world security studies at Hampshire College and the author of *Resource Wars: The New Landscape of Global Conflict*.

As you read, consider the following questions:

1. Why did the Cheney Report become infamous, in the author's opinion?
2. According to Klare, why is the United States increasingly involved in Colombia's civil war?
3. What two alternatives to military involvement does the author argue might better help the United States meet its energy needs?

Since its inception, the Bush Administration has launched two great foreign policy initiatives: a global war against terrorism, and a global campaign to expand American access to foreign oil. Originally, each possessed its own rationale and mode of operation. As time has passed, however, they have become increasingly intertwined, so that today the war on terrorism and the struggle for oil have become one vast enterprise.

The underpinnings of the Bush foreign policy can be found in the national energy policy paper of May 17, 2001, known as the Cheney report. This report became infamous for two reasons: [Vice President Dick] Cheney wouldn't release the names of the people he consulted for it, and the report recommends drilling in the Arctic National Wildlife Refuge. But these controversies distracted attention away from the gist of the report, which is spelled out in chapter eight, "Strengthening Global Alliances." There, the report "recommends that the President make energy security a priority of our trade and foreign policy."

The report says the United States will become increasingly reliant on foreign oil. At present, we obtain about half of our petroleum from foreign sources; by 2020, imports will account for two-thirds of U.S. consumption, the report predicts. From this, it draws two conclusions: The United States must maintain good relations with Saudi Arabia and other oil producers in the region, and the United States must diversify oil suppliers around the world. "Middle East oil producers will remain central to world oil security," it says, but "our engagement must be global." This means developing close ties with major suppliers in all oil-producing areas, including the Caspian region, Africa, and Latin America, which the report calls "high-priority areas."

The United States Needs Saudi Oil

The Administration was already poised to act on this policy when Arab hijackers struck New York and Washington on September 11 [2001]. These plans were then put aside, as the White House concentrated its attention on efforts to immobilize Al Qaeda [terrorists, who were responsible for the attack] and to topple the Taliban regime in Afghanistan [which was harboring Al Qaeda]. By December, however, the Administration was ready to focus again on the security aspects of growing U.S. dependence on imported oil.

The primacy of oil is clear in several places, most obviously, Saudi Arabia. Though fifteen of the eighteen hijackers were Saudi, though [September 11 mastermind] Osama bin Laden himself is Saudi, though the Saudis practice Wahhabism [a fundamentalist form of Islam] and finance some of the most reactionary madrassas [fundamentalist Islamic schools] around the world, the Bush Administration is in no position to break relations with the kingdom. Saudi Arabia possesses 25 percent of the world's known oil reserves. And, as the Cheney report notes, "Saudi Arabia, the world's largest exporter, has been a linchpin of supply reliability to world oil markets." It seems Washington has embraced the current Middle East peace initiative by Prince Abdullah of Saudi Arabia as a way . . . to shore up the reputation of this crucial ally.

Or look at the U.S. military training operation in the Republic of Georgia, which is just getting under way. Ostensibly, the aim of the operation—which will involve the deployment of several hundred U.S. Special Forces advisers—is to enhance the capacity of Georgian forces to fight terrorists and other insurgents along its border. While this is certainly one of the operation's objectives, it is also evident that Washington seeks to reduce the threat to the vital pipelines that will carry oil from the Caspian Sea across Georgia to ports on the Black Sea and the Mediterranean. Although the main pipeline is still under construction, U.S. officials are clearly worried that it will become a major target for the various ethnic militias that operate in the area.

Anti-Terror and Oil-Supply Missions Merge

"The Caspian Sea can also be a rapidly growing new area of supply," the Cheney report notes. "Proven oil reserves in Azerbaijan and Kazakhstan are about twenty billion barrels, a little more than the North Sea." One find in Kazakhstan, it adds, is "comparable to Prudhoe Bay," the giant oil field off the north coast of Alaska. Its recommendation to the President: "Ensure that rising Caspian oil production is effectively integrated into world oil trade." One way it is doing this, in the wake of September 11, is to establish perma-

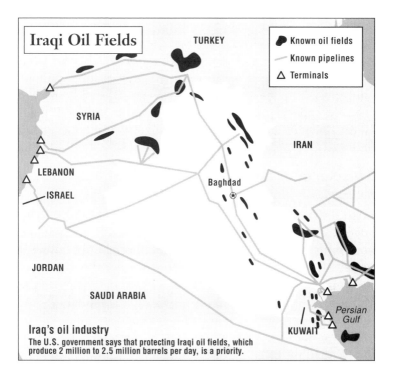

Iraqi Oil Fields

TURKEY

● Known oil fields
— Known pipelines
△ Terminals

SYRIA

IRAN

LEBANON

Baghdad

ISRAEL

JORDAN

SAUDI ARABIA

Persian Gulf

KUWAIT

Iraq's oil industry
The U.S. government says that protecting Iraqi oil fields, which produce 2 million to 2.5 million barrels per day, is a priority.

nent bases in Tajikistan, Uzbekistan, and Kyrgyzstan.

A similar situation is developing in Colombia. The United States has increasingly involved itself in Colombia's civil war, first on the pretext of fighting the war on drugs. (Both the leftwing guerrillas and the rightwing paramilitaries are involved in the drug trade, but the United States shows little interest in the paramilitaries.) Increasingly, the Bush Administration is seeking to aid the Colombian military directly in its war against the guerrilla groups—often described as terrorists by U.S. and Colombian officials. In the latest incarnation of this effort, the United States will help the Colombian military to protect the pipeline that delivers oil from Occidental Petroleum's Cano Limon oilfield to refineries and terminals on the coast—a pipeline the rebels have often sabotaged.

Several factors are facilitating the merger of the anti-terror and oil-supply missions. The first is geography: Many of the world's largest reserves of oil are located in areas that are unstable or rent by internal divisions of one sort or another.

The second is growing U.S. dependency on imported oil. As domestic reserves are progressively depleted, the United States will become increasingly reliant on oil derived from sources located abroad. At the same time, world demand for oil, especially from the developing nations, will grow, the Cheney report notes, which could push prices higher. "Growth in international oil demand will exert increasing pressure on global oil availability," it notes.

The Need for Oil Does Not Justify Military Action

With the American public fixated on the threat of terrorism, however, the Administration is understandably reluctant to portray its foreign policy as related primarily to the protection of oil supplies. Thus the third reason for the merger of the war against terrorism and struggle for oil: to provide the White House with a convenient rationale for extending U.S. military involvement into areas that are of concern to Washington primarily because of their role in supplying energy to the United States.

For all of these reasons, the war against terrorism and the struggle for oil are likely to remain connected for the indefinite future. This will entail growing U.S. military involvement in the oil-supplying nations. At times, such involvement may be limited to indirect forms of assistance, such as arms transfers and training programs. At others, it will involve the deployment of significant numbers of U.S. combat troops.

The Bush Administration has a right and an obligation to take the necessary steps to protect the United States against further acts of terrorism. Such efforts have been given unequivocal support by the public and Congress. But such support does not extend to an open-ended campaign to procure additional oil from overseas suppliers and to protect these supplies from hostile forces.

Before committing additional military resources to such an effort, we should consider if America's energy requirements could be better provided through conservation and alternative energy systems, which would reduce the risk of U.S. involvement in an endless series of overseas conflicts.

"The contention that the . . . war is really about oil is senseless as well as being baseless."

The War on Terrorism Is Not a Struggle for Oil

Peter Ferrara

Peter Ferrara argues in the following viewpoint that America's war on terrorism in Iraq in 2003 would not be fought to ensure a steady supply of Iraqi oil as some critics of the war claim. He maintains that there is no need to go to war for oil, since the United States will ultimately get all the oil it needs from Iraq through world oil markets. Indeed, he points out, Iraq's oil supplies are of no value to that nation unless it can sell oil to America. Peter Ferrara is director of the International Center for Law and Economics in Fairfax, Virginia.

As you read, consider the following questions:
1. Who is responsible for the claim that war with Iraq is about oil rather than terrorism, according to Ferrara?
2. In the author's opinion, what would happen if oil producers tried to cut off the huge U.S. consumer market?
3. According to Ferrara, why is the U.S. oil boycott against Iraq no real threat?

Peter Ferrara, "It's Not About the Oil, Already," www.nationalreview.com, February 21, 2003. Copyright © 2003 by National Review, Inc. Reproduced by permission of United Feature Syndicate, Inc.

The American Left and its international comrades are claiming that the [2003] war with Iraq is not about de-fanging terrorism.[1] Rather, they say, it's all about oil. They argue that President [George W.] Bush is really motivated by a desire to seize Iraqi oil for American oil companies (and gas-guzzling American SUV drivers). "No blood for oil!" is their rallying cry.

No basis has ever been cited for this accusation—perhaps because the accusation makes no sense, as a matter of basic economics.

Unless the Iraqis drill and sell their oil, it is worthless to them. They must sell it somewhere on the world oil market to get any gain out of it.

But oil is a fungible commodity, so once they sell it—any-where—it becomes part of the world oil supply. That in-creased supply in turn reduces the world oil price, until some equilibrium is reached between supply and demand.

From that point on, it doesn't matter to anyone where the Iraqi oil actually goes. If it goes to Japan, the Japanese will buy less oil from Venezuela and Nigeria. More oil from those countries would then go to the U.S. Indeed, as the oil supply sloshes around on world markets, no one really cares—or keeps track of—where it originated, so long as it meets qual-ity standards. For all anybody knows or cares, every drop of Iraqi oil could end up at southern California gas stations.

Americans Buy Most of the World's Oil

Moreover, just who do the "war protesters" think Iraq would sell its oil to, in any event? The Western oil companies, pri-marily American companies, would be the primary pur-chasers of Iraqi oil, whether they buy it directly or cir-cuitously through various middlemen. Who else is going to refine, distribute, and sell the stuff to the huge Western (and particularly American) consumer market? Have you ever seen or heard of any Iraqi gas stations?

In short, the oil companies already ultimately get the oil *now*. They don't need Bush to go to war to get it for them.

---

1. The Bush administration claimed that the war in Iraq was necessary because Iraq was developing weapons of mass destruction and aiding anti-American terrorists.

The proportion of the world oil supply currently consumed by America will continue to get here one way or another through world oil markets. If oil producers tried to cut off the huge American consumer market, there would effectively be a huge drop in the total world demand for their oil —and, consequently, a huge reduction in the world price.

The War Against Iraq Is Not About Oil

The charge [that the war on terrorism is a war for oil] has a surface plausibility because Iraq does have the second-largest known reserves in the world. But we certainly don't need to send 250,000 soldiers to get at it. [Iraqi leader] Saddam Hussein would gladly sell us all the oil we wanted. The only thing preventing unlimited sales are the United States-enforced sanctions, which Baghdad (and the big oil companies) would love to see lifted. Washington has refused to go along because Saddam Hussein flouts United Nations resolutions. This suggests that our primary focus is the threat he poses, not the oil he possesses.

Max Boot, *New York Times*, February 13, 2003.

Who else is going to consume world oil output *except* American consumers (and those gas-guzzling SUVs)? The truth is that Middle Eastern oil producers—including Iraq— need America and its consumers a lot more than we need them. We can always figure out other ways of powering our transportation and warming our homes, technologically. But has the Middle East ever figured out any way of getting dollars other than pumping and selling oil?

That is why an oil boycott is ultimately no real threat either. Again, Iraq and other oil producers must sell the oil somewhere on the world market to get anything out of it. And once they do, they add to the world oil supply and reduce the price to approach a new supply/demand equilibrium. The world oil market then distributes the available oil supply to wherever the demand is—which means America and the rest of the West.

Indeed, it is the West that has been restraining Iraqi oil supply since the Gulf War, with various restrictions on Iraqi oil sales. And it has been the Iraqis who have been pleading to open up their production and sales. An Iraqi oil boycott is not even remotely an issue today.

So the contention that the . . . war is really about oil is senseless as well as being baseless. Which leaves us with this question: Why is the American Left joining with its foreign comrades to defame America with this silly and transparently false accusation? Is it really all just about anti-Americanism? Is it really just rooted in a hatred of American power and an attempt to stop its exercise? Isn't it time they came clean and told the truth?

"The so-called War on Terror was always just an expedient reason for the unilateral use of military power to achieve global dominance."

The War on Terrorism Is Being Fought to Expand U.S. World Dominance

Jim Lobe

In the following viewpoint Jim Lobe maintains that the September 11, 2001, terrorist attacks on the United States provided neoconservatives—those who believe that the United States should use its military power to manage global order—with an excuse to begin a push for worldwide dominance. Further, he argues that it is this desire for global dominance rather than the threat of terrorism that drives the war. Jim Lobe writes for Inter Press Service, an international newswire, and for Foreign Policy in Focus, a joint project of the Institute for Policy Studies and the Interhemispheric Resource Center.

As you read, consider the following questions:
1. According to the author, what did the draft of the Defense Planning Guidance indicate the role of the U.S. military should be?
2. The author argues that traditionally U.S. foreign policy was based on what two broad strategies?
3. What key attitudes do neoconservatives share, in Lobe's opinion?

Jim Lobe, "The Anniversary of the Neo-Imperial Movement," *AlterNet*, September 12, 2002. Copyright © 2003 by *AlterNet*. Reproduced by permission.

When excerpts of the document first appeared in the *New York Times* in the spring of 1992, it created quite a stir. Sen. Joe Biden, now chairman of the Senate Foreign Relations Committee was particularly outraged, calling it a prescription for "literally a Pax Americana," an American empire.

The details contained in the draft of the Defense Planning Guidance (DPG) were indeed startling.

The document argued that the core assumption guiding U.S. foreign policy in the 21st century should be the need to establish permanent U.S. dominance over virtually all of Eurasia.

It envisioned a world in which U.S. military intervention would become "a constant fixture" of the geo-political landscape. "While the U.S. cannot become the world's 'policeman' by assuming responsibility for righting every wrong, we will retain the preeminent responsibility for addressing selectively those wrongs which threaten not only our interests, but those of our allies or friends," wrote the authors, Paul Wolfowitz and I. Lewis Libby—who at the time were two relatively obscure political appointees in the Pentagon's policy office.

The strategies put forward to achieve this goal included "deterring potential competitors from even aspiring to a larger regional or global role," and taking pre-emptive action against states suspected of developing weapons of mass destruction.

The draft, leaked apparently by a high-ranking source in the military, sparked an intense but fleeting uproar. At the insistence of then–National Security Adviser Brent Scowcroft and Secretary of State James Baker, the final DPG document was toned down beyond recognition.

But through the nineties, the two authors and their boss, then–Pentagon chief Dick Cheney, continued to wait for the right opportunity to fulfill their imperial dreams.

Their long wait came to an end on the morning of Sept. 11, 2001, when two hijacked commercial airliners slammed into the World Trade Center towers in Manhattan and a third into the Pentagon outside Washington.

And the timing could not have been more ideal. Dick Cheney had already become the most powerful vice president in U.S. history, while the draft's two authors, Wolfowitz and Libby, were now Deputy Defense Secretary and Cheney's chief of staff and national security adviser, respectively.

The Desire for Global Dominance Drives Foreign Policy

In the year since, these three men, along with Defense Secretary Donald Rumsfeld and like-minded officials strategically located elsewhere in the administration, have engineered what former U.N. Ambassador Richard Holbrooke recently described as a "radical break with 55 years of bipartisan tradition" in U.S. foreign policy.

U.S. foreign policy after World War II was based on two broad strategies: a realist policy organized around containment and deterrence to U.S. power; and a more liberal, internationalist policy based on the construction of a set of multilateral institutions and alliances to promote open market-based economies and democratic values.

While Republican administrations leaned more towards the realist agenda and Democratic administrations toward the internationalist perspective, neither deviated very far from the core assumptions.

But now, "[f]or the first time since the dawn of the Cold War, a new grand strategy is taking shape in Washington," says Georgetown University professor G. John Ikenberry. In his article 'America's Imperial Ambition' published in the [September 2002] edition of *Foreign Affairs*, he argues that the Bush administration's foreign policy since Sept. 11 is driven by the desire for global dominance rather than the threat of terrorism.

"According to this new paradigm, America is to be less bound to its partners and to global rules and institutions while it steps forward to play a more unilateral and anticipatory role in attacking terrorist threats and confronting rogue states seeking WMD (weapons of mass destruction)," Ikenberry writes. "The United States will use its unrivaled military power to manage the global order."

Advocates of the new paradigm are part of a coalition of three major political forces, which include right-wing Machtpolitikers, like Rumsfeld and Cheney, mainly Jewish neo-conservatives closely tied to the Likud Party in Israel, and leaders of the Christian and Catholic Right.

A War to Guarantee U.S. Dominance

Looking closely, we see that the [September 11, 2001, terrorist attacks on the United States] gave the Bush Administration the political opening to attempt to impose its will militarily, to massively increase military spending and weapons acquisition, to advance its right-wing domestic agenda, and to exercise an arrogance of power that was beyond our imaginations.

How did this happen? At the popular level, the 9-11 attacks plunged the country into a dangerous identity crisis. For the first time in almost 200 years, the two great oceans were not vast enough to protect U.S. citizens from attack. The losses and pain suffered by many people have been amplified and manipulated by the president and his mandarins who are no strangers to Machiavelli, by the mass media, by politicians, by the U.S. military-industrial-complex, by religious fundamentalists and racist authoritarians, and by our culture of U.S. exceptionalism. This has been compounded by the erosion of democratic values, practices and structures over the past generation.

The Bush Administration, is using this confusion and disorientation, and the United States' enormous military and economic power, to create a New New World Order to guarantee U.S. dominance far into the 21st century. [Secretary of State] Colin Powell put it well when he said that the 9-11 attacks "set the reset button" on U.S. foreign and military policies.

Joseph Gerson, from a speech given to the Taking Our Message Home conference, March 16, 2002.

The events of Sept. 11 effectively empowered this coalition within the Bush administration at the expense of the more-traditional realists led by Secretary of State Colin Powell, who, significantly, has received strong support from veterans of the first Bush administration, most prominently Brent Scowcroft and James Baker.

Aside from a strong belief in U.S. military power, these men share a number of key attitudes that shape their foreign policy prescriptives. These include a contempt for multilateralism which necessarily denies the "exceptional" nature of the United States; a similar disdain and distrust for Europeans, especially the French; and a conviction that "fundamentalist" Islam poses a major threat to the United States and the West. They also consider China a long-term strategic threat that should be confronted sooner rather than later.

The So-Called War on Terror Is an Excuse

And these views have shaped the White House's policy decisions including its strong support of Israeli Prime Minister Ariel Sharon and its attack on various multilateral institutions, such as the International Criminal Court (ICC), and key arms-control accords, like the 1972 Anti-Ballistic Missile (ABM) treaty, not to mention its push for a war on Iraq and "regime change" in a number of Middle Eastern countries, including Saudi Arabia.

In other words, U.S. foreign policy today looks and sounds remarkably like the DPG draft leaked nearly ten years ago.

On this anniversary of Sept. 11 [2001], it is increasingly clear that Cheney and his proteges have used the tragedy to validate their dangerous delusions of grandeur. The so-called War on Terror was always just an expedient reason for the unilateral use of military power to achieve global dominance.

"The advance of freedom is the calling of our time; it is the calling of our country."

The War on Terrorism Is Being Fought to Foster Democracy Worldwide

George W. Bush

In the spring of 2003, the United States toppled Iraqi leader Saddam Hussein, who the Bush administration claimed was developing weapons of mass destruction and aiding anti-American terrorists. The Iraq war was part of America's larger war against terrorism in the aftermath of the September 11, 2001, terrorist attacks. President George W. Bush argues in the following viewpoint, originally given as a speech before the National Endowment for Democracy on November 6, 2003, that the U.S. war on terrorism will provide opportunities to help the countries in the Middle East and elsewhere achieve a democratic form of government and the peace and freedom that flow from it. Moreover, he maintains that while establishing democracy in the Middle East will require continued sacrifice, it is the destiny of the United States to lead this fight for freedom.

As you read, consider the following questions:

1. According to the author, how many democracies were there in the world in the early 1970s?
2. In Bush's opinion, what does the advance of freedom lead to?
3. What does the author argue are the essential principles common to every successful society?

George W. Bush, address at the Twentieth Anniversary of the National Endowment for Democracy, U.S. Chamber of Commerce, Washington, DC, November 6, 2003.

Thanks for inviting me to join you in this 20th anniversary of the National Endowment for Democracy. The staff and directors of this organization have seen a lot of history over the last two decades, you've been a part of that history. By speaking for and standing for freedom, you've lifted the hopes of people around the world, and you've brought great credit to America. . . .

The roots of our democracy can be traced to England, and to its Parliament—and so can the roots of this organization. In June of 1982, President Ronald Reagan spoke at Westminster Palace and declared, the turning point had arrived in history. He argued that Soviet communism had failed, precisely because it did not respect its own people—their creativity, their genius and their rights.

President Reagan said that the day of Soviet tyranny was passing, that freedom had a momentum which would not be halted. He gave this organization its mandate: to add to the momentum of freedom across the world. Your mandate was important 20 years ago; it is equally important today. . . .

The great democratic movement President Reagan described was already well underway. In the early 1970s, there were about 40 democracies in the world. By the middle of that decade, Portugal and Spain and Greece held free elections. Soon there were new democracies in Latin America, and free institutions were spreading in Korea, in Taiwan, and in East Asia. This very week in 1989, there were protests in East Berlin and in Leipzig. By the end of that year, every communist dictatorship in Central Europe had collapsed. Within another year, the South African government released Nelson Mandela. Four years later, he was elected president of his country—ascending, . . . from prisoner of state to head of state.

The United States Fueled World Democracy

As the 20th century ended, there were around 120 democracies in the world—and I can assure you more are on the way. Ronald Reagan would be pleased, and he would not be surprised.

We've witnessed, in little over a generation, the swiftest advance of freedom in the 2,500 year story of democracy.

Historians in the future will offer their own explanations for why this happened. Yet we already know some of the reasons they will cite. It is no accident that the rise of so many democracies took place in a time when the world's most influential nation was itself a democracy. . . .

The United States Seeks Democracy for Iraq

If we profess support for democracy in Iraq now, before the bombs fall, this assurance to the Iraqi people may help our cause more than a European armored division or a Middle Eastern base. Our commitment to political reform [in that nation, which was targeted as a terrorist threat]—not to any individual or clique—will give us the military and ethical advantage of consistency, purpose, and clarity.

Americans hope for constitutional governments in the Middle East not because we are naive, but because we seek democracy's practical dividends. Modern democracies rarely attack America or each other. When they fight illiberal regimes, they win. The Falklands, Panama, Serbia, and the Middle East all demonstrate the power of legitimate governments over dictatorships. Yet this pragmatic consideration is often dismissed as starry-eyed idealism. Only belatedly have we advocated democratic reform for the Palestinians, as a remedy for our previous failed policy of appeasement of [Yassir] Arafat and his corrupt regime.

We are not talking of Jeffersonian democracy all at once. First, remove the dictator, to permit a more lawful society to evolve on the model of Panama, Grenada, Serbia, and the Philippines. Keep up the pressure of American and world opinion, international aid, the return of Westernized dissidents, the emancipation of women, and the occasional threat of American force. Let [the terrorist attacks of] September 11 [2001] remind us that inaction can be as deadly as intervention.

Victor Davis Hanson, *Weekly Standard*, October 21, 2002.

The progress of liberty is a powerful trend. Yet, we also know that liberty, if not defended, can be lost. The success of freedom is not determined by some dialectic of history. By definition, the success of freedom rests upon the choices and the courage of free peoples, and upon their willingness to sacrifice. In the trenches of World War I, through a two-front war in the 1940s, the difficult battles of Korea and

Vietnam, and in missions of rescue and liberation on nearly every continent, Americans have amply displayed our willingness to sacrifice for liberty.

The sacrifices of Americans have not always been recognized or appreciated, yet they have been worthwhile. Because we and our allies were steadfast, Germany and Japan are democratic nations that no longer threaten the world. A global nuclear standoff with the Soviet Union ended peacefully—as did the Soviet Union. The nations of Europe are moving towards unity, not dividing into armed camps and descending into genocide. Every nation has learned, or should have learned, an important lesson: Freedom is worth fighting for, dying for, and standing for—and the advance of freedom leads to peace.

And now we must apply that lesson in our own time. We've reached another great turning point—and the resolve we show will shape the next stage of the world democratic movement . . .

Our commitment to democracy is . . . tested in the Middle East, which is my focus today, and must be a focus of American policy for decades to come. In many nations of the Middle East—countries of great strategic importance—democracy has not yet taken root. And the questions arise: Are the peoples of the Middle East somehow beyond the reach of liberty? Are millions of men and women and children condemned by history or culture to live in despotism? Are they alone never to know freedom, and never even to have a choice in the matter? I, for one, do not believe it. I believe every person has the ability and the right to be free. . . .

Islam Is Consistent with Democracy

It should be clear to all that Islam—the faith of one-fifth of humanity—is consistent with democratic rule. Democratic progress is found in many predominantly Muslim countries—in Turkey and Indonesia, and Senegal and Albania, Niger and Sierra Leone. Muslim men and women are good citizens of India and South Africa, of the nations of Western Europe, and of the United States of America.

More than half of all the Muslims in the world live in freedom under democratically constituted governments. They succeed in democratic societies, not in spite of their faith, but because of it. A religion that demands individual moral accountability, and encourages the encounter of the individual with God, is fully compatible with the rights and responsibilities of self-government.

Yet there's a great challenge today in the Middle East. In the words of a recent report by Arab scholars, the global wave of democracy has—and I quote—"barely reached the Arab states." They continue: "This freedom deficit undermines human development and is one of the most painful manifestations of lagging political development." The freedom deficit they describe has terrible consequences, of the people of the Middle East and for the world. In many Middle Eastern countries, poverty is deep and it is spreading, women lack rights and are denied schooling. Whole societies remain stagnant while the world moves ahead. These are not the failures of a culture or a religion. These are the failures of political and economic doctrines. . . .

Many Middle Eastern governments now understand that military dictatorship and theocratic rule are a straight, smooth highway to nowhere. But some governments still cling to the old habits of central control. There are governments that still fear and repress independent thought and creativity, and private enterprise—the human qualities that make for—strong and successful societies. Even when these nations have vast natural resources, they do not respect or develop their greatest resources—the talent and energy of men and women working and living in freedom. . . .

Reform Is Critical to the Middle East

As changes come to the Middle Eastern region, those with power should ask themselves: Will they be remembered for resisting reform, or for leading it? In Iran, the demand for democracy is strong and broad, as we saw . . . when thousands gathered to welcome home Shirin Ebadi, the winner of the Nobel Peace Prize. The regime in Teheran must heed the democratic demands of the Iranian people, or lose its last claim to legitimacy.

For the Palestinian people, the only path to independence and dignity and progress is the path of democracy. And the

Palestinian leaders who block and undermine democratic reform, and feed hatred and encourage violence are not leaders at all. They're the main obstacles to peace, and to the success of the Palestinian people.

The Saudi government is taking first steps toward reform, including a plan for gradual introduction of elections. By giving the Saudi people a greater role in their own society, the Saudi government can demonstrate true leadership in the region.

The great and proud nation of Egypt has shown the way toward peace in the Middle East, and now should show the way toward democracy in the Middle East. Champions of democracy in the region understand that democracy is not perfect, it is not the path to utopia, but it's the only path to national success and dignity.

As we watch and encourage reforms in the region, we are mindful that modernization is not the same as Westernization. Representative governments in the Middle East will reflect their own cultures. They will not, and should not, look like us. Democratic nations may be constitutional monarchies, federal republics, or parliamentary systems. And working democracies always need time to develop—as did our own. We've taken a 200-year journey toward inclusion and justice—and this makes us patient and understanding as other nations are at different stages of this journey.

There are, however, essential principles common to every successful society, in every culture. Successful societies limit the power of the state and the power of the military—so that governments respond to the will of the people, and not the will of an elite. Successful societies protect freedom with the consistent and impartial rule of law, instead of . . . selectively applying the law to punish political opponents. Successful societies allow room for healthy civic institutions—for political parties and labor unions and independent newspapers and broadcast media. Successful societies guarantee religious liberty—the right to serve and honor God without fear of persecution. Successful societies privatize their economies, and secure the rights of property. They prohibit and punish official corruption, and invest in the health and education of their people. They recognize the rights of women. And instead of directing hatred and resentment against others, successful societies appeal to the hopes of their own people. . . .

The Advance of Democracy Is America's Calling

In Iraq, the Coalition Provisional Authority and the Iraqi Governing Council are also working together to build a democracy—and after three decades of tyranny, this work is not easy.[1] The former dictator ruled by terror and treachery, and left deeply ingrained habits of fear and distrust. Remnants of his regime, joined by foreign terrorists, continue their battle against order and against civilization. Our coalition is responding to recent attacks with precision raids, guided by intelligence provided by the Iraqis, themselves. And we're working closely with Iraqi citizens as they prepare a constitution, as they move toward free elections and take increasing responsibility for their own affairs. As in the defense of Greece in 1947, and later in the Berlin Airlift, the strength and will of free peoples are now being tested before a watching world. And we will meet this test.

Securing democracy in Iraq is the work of many hands. American and coalition forces are sacrificing for the peace of Iraq and for the security of free nations. Aid workers from many countries are facing danger to help the Iraqi people. The National Endowment for Democracy is promoting women's rights, and training Iraqi journalists, and teaching the skills of political participation. Iraqis, themselves—police and borders guards and local officials—are joining in the work and they are sharing in the sacrifice.

This is a massive and difficult undertaking—it is worth our effort, it is worth our sacrifice, because we know the stakes. The failure of Iraqi democracy would embolden terrorists around the world, increase dangers to the American people, and extinguish the hopes of millions in the region. Iraqi democracy will succeed—and that success will send forth the news, from Damascus to Teheran—that freedom can be the future of every nation. The establishment of a

---

1. The Bush administration claimed that the 2003 war in Iraq was necessary to topple Iraqi leader Saddam Hussein, who was developing weapons of mass destruction and aiding anti-American terrorists. The war was part of America's larger war against terrorism.

free Iraq at the heart of the Middle East will be a watershed event in the global democratic revolution. . . .

Therefore, the United States has adopted a new policy, a forward strategy of freedom in the Middle East. This strategy requires the same persistence and energy and idealism we have shown before. And it will yield the same results. As in Europe, as in Asia, as in every region of the world, the advance of freedom leads to peace.

The advance of freedom is the calling of our time; it is the calling of our country. . . . America has put our power at the service of principle. We believe that liberty is the design of nature; we believe that liberty is the direction of history. We believe that human fulfillment and excellence come in the responsible exercise of liberty. And we believe that freedom— the freedom we prize—is not for us alone, it is the right and the capacity of all mankind.

> *"The threat posed by Saddam Hussein's regime and its unmistakable alliance with al-Qaeda . . . posed a clear and present danger . . . to the United States."*

The War in Iraq Was Justified

Dan Darling

In the spring of 2003, the United States went to war with Iraq to depose Iraqi leader Saddam Hussein, whom the Bush administration accused of aiding terrorists. Dan Darling maintains in the following viewpoint that Iraq presented an imminent threat to the United States, justifying the war. Darling insists that Iraq is tacitly linked to the terrorist group al Qaeda, and that Hussein provided the terrorist organization with the support it needed to carry out attacks against the United States and several western European nations. Further, he argues specifically that the terrorist Abu Musab Zarqawi (Al-Zarqawi) was in collusion with the Iraqi government in planning terrorist activities. Dan Darling is a writer for Winds of Change.Net, a Web site providing commentary on national and global events.

As you read, consider the following questions:
1. According to the author, what did al Qaeda informants say Iraq agreed to do to help them?
2. Who was the first al Qaeda leader to attack Israel directly, in Darling's opinion?
3. What does Darling maintain is the link between terrorist cells in London, Paris, and Catalonia?

Whether one supported or opposed the [2003] war in Iraq, one of the questions that has been raised in both liberal and conservative circles since the fall of Saddam Hussein's regime is whether or not Iraq posed a sufficient threat to the United States and its allies to justify such an invasion.

This analysis will attempt to argue that the threat posed by Saddam Hussein's regime and its unmistakeable alliance with [the terrorist group] al-Qaeda[1] was such that it posed a clear and present danger not only to the United States but also to some of fiercest opponents of the war—the populations of Western Europe. Much of this information is already on public record and was summarized by US Secretary of State Colin Powell in his presentation before the United Nations, but this is the first such presentation to my knowledge to make the allegation that Abu Musab Zarqawi was in active collusion with the government of Saddam Hussein in orchestrating his terrorist activities.

Before I begin, it is imperative to point out that revisionist history to the contrary, claims of some type of tactical relationship between al-Qaeda and Iraq are hardly new. Indeed, one can simply examine this story on the BBC website (hardly the most pro-American source) from October 2000 in which former CIA counter-terrorism chief Vincent Cannistraro states unequivocally that al-Qaeda was in contact with the Iraqi military and not a word about the "incompatability" of ideologies or the alleged hatred that [al-Qaeda leader Osama] bin Laden feels for Saddam Hussein.

Link Between Saddam and al-Qaeda

But the first signs that the relationship between Saddam Hussein and al-Qaeda was far more than a tactical one appears to have been uncovered following the fall of [Afghanistan's] Taliban and capture of numerous members of the organization's leadership [who were harboring al-Qaeda members]. At some point during the interrogations of al-Qaeda's leaders, one of the training camp commanders claimed that Iraq agreed to assist the organization with the development of chemical and biological weapons as far back as December 2000. While it is

1. Al-Qaeda masterminded the September 11, 2001, terrorist attacks on America.

unclear which of the al-Qaeda leaders now in custody made this claim to the US, a partial listing of the group's leadership leaves us with two potential sources: Ibn al-Shaykh al-Libi and Abd al-Hadi al-Iraqi.

From the looks of things, there appears to have been more than just two terrorists' good word to back these claims up; US forces in Afghanistan found traces of anthrax and ricin at the organization's biological weapons sites in Afghanistan. These claims are further bolstered by the testimony of CIA Director George Tenet in February 2003.

In mid-2002, Abu Musab Zarqawi arrived in Baghdad from Iran and received medical treatment there before heading north to join Ansar al-Islam. According to Secretary of State Colin Powell's presentation before the United Nations, shortly after Zarqawi's arrival in Baghdad over two dozen al-Qaeda operatives coverged on Baghdad and were apparently able to remain there at the behest of the Iraqi regime. This claim can be corroborated by reports that Saddam Hussein had created a "safe zone" for al-Qaeda within his territory at about the same time that Zarqawi left Baghdad for northern Iraq.

In northern Iraq, Zarqawi and his lieutenants in Ansar al-Islam soon began testing ricin as well as other chemical weapons. These crude chemical weapons eventually made their way to Europe, a point I'll touch more on in a moment.

Zarqawi also appears to have been the first al-Qaeda leader to attack Israel directly. In September 2002, Israeli radio reported the arrest of three Palestinian al-Qaeda operatives who had been trained in Iraq, presumably by Ansar al-Islam.

A US Diplomat Was Assassinated

As I noted in my earlier Zarqawi analysis, while in northern Iraq he ordered the assassination of US diplomat Lawrence Foley in Jordan. It is worth noting that one of Foley's killers, a Libyan national named Salem bin Suweid, is a probable member of the Libyan Islamic Fighting Group and had had poison files on his computers. Zarqawi's deputy, Moammar Ahmed Yousef, oversaw the killing from Syria but was later detained. According to an article in the UK *Independent* that I am still trying to locate online, it was this deputy's capture

Abu Musab Zarqawi's Iraq-Linked Terrorist Network

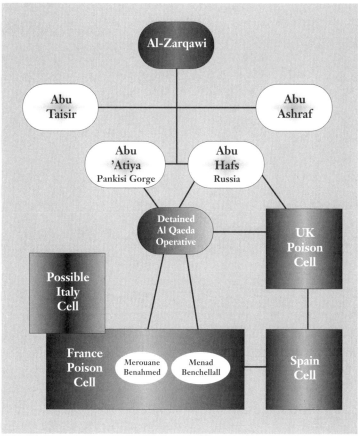

Colin L. Powell, "Remarks to the United Nations Security Council," February 5, 2003.

that enabled the US to learn a great deal about al-Qaeda's ties with the Iraqi regime.

On November 12 of 2002 al-Jazeera [Arab television station] broadcast a purported audiotape of Osama bin Laden claiming responsibility for a string of terrorist attacks that included the Foley assassination. Within less than a week, three Algerian al-Qaeda operatives were arrested plotting to release cyanide in the London Underground [subway system]. Over the course of the next three months, other al-Qaeda cells in Europe were disrupted in Paris and Catalonia, as well as the discovery of a ricin lab in North London. What did all of these cells have in common? They all received training and marching orders from two al-Qaeda leaders—Abu Khabab, the organization's top WMD [weapons of mass destruction] specialist, and Abu Musab Zarqawi.

What does all of this mean as far as the threat from Iraq is concerned? The Algerian operatives who planned to use ricin to attack the UK were trained by Ansar al-Islam. Among Ansar al-Islam's leadership, according to no less respectable a source than *Time Magazine* was one of Saddam Hussein's agents. According to the *Kurdistan Observer* and other sources, the real leader of Ansar al-Islam is Abu Wael, who is apparently one and the same as the Mukhabarat agent referenced in *Time Magazine*.

So what does this all mean to those unfamiliar with the murky world of international terrorism? An Algerian terrorist aligned with al-Qaeda under the command of Abu Musab Zarqawi and Abu Khabab attempted to use chemical weapons to attack European (as well as Russian and US targets according to the State Department) targets between November 2002 and January 2003. Had any one of these attacks succeeded, it is likely that significant numbers of innocent people would have lost their lives. Most of these attacks were planned from northern Iraq by Ansar al-Islam. None of these facts are in dispute.

Saddam Hussein's Rule

If one assumes that there was a link between Saddam Hussein and Ansar al-Islam to the point where one of his agents was, knowingly or unknowingly, the *de facto* leader of the organization. Assuming Abu Wael had some means by which to communicate with his superiors in the Iraqi Mukhabarat, this means that the Mukhabarat was likely aware of what was going on but made no effort to stop it or to inform the UK, France, or Spain of what was taking place, let alone Russia or the US. That makes Saddam for all practical purposes complicit in these attempted attacks, especially if his relationship with Ansar al-Islam was as cozy in December 2002 as the Iraqi opposition claims it was, while the would-be attacks in Europe were ongoing.

As Colin Powell said at the United Nations: "Terrorism has been a tool used by Saddam for decades. Saddam was a supporter of terrorism long before these terrorist networks had a name. And this support continues. The nexus of poisons and terror is new. The nexus of Iraq and terror is old. The combination is lethal."

Indeed. The is much more on what has been learned or can be plausibly discerned from the evidence accumulated to date that Stephen F. Hayes laid out in a recent article in the *Weekly Standard.* However, my purpose writing this analysis is to explain that the regime of Saddam Hussein harbored and provided tacit if not active support to a terrorist organization that attempted to kill hundreds if not thousands of innocent people [in 2002]. Such an action constitutes a clear example of an imminent threat to US if not global security and is in of itself a clear and rational if not moral justification for removing the Baathist regime from power.

"It was not necessary to go to war at this time, in this place."

The War in Iraq Was Not Justified

Joseph Cirincione

In the following viewpoint Joseph Cirincione argues that the Iraq war was fought because of a false assertion, made by the Bush administration, that Saddam Hussein was responsible for the September 11, 2001, terrorist attacks on the United States. However, no evidence exists linking Hussein with the attacks, he maintains. According to Cirincione, Bush administration officials simply want to increase U.S. presence in the Middle East and want to take over Iraq so they can use that nation as their base of operations. Joseph Cirincione is a senior associate and director of the Non-Proliferation Project at the Carnegie Endowment for International Peace in Washington, D.C.

As you read, consider the following questions:

1. According to the author, what treaty did President John F. Kennedy start negotiating?
2. How many countries have nuclear weapons, in the author's opinion?
3. According to Cirincione, what does the Project for the New American Century say about Iraq?

Joseph Cirincione, speech at American University, Washington, DC, March 22, 2003, Veterans Against the Iraq War–sponsored "Teach-In & Speak Out Against Iraq War," C-SPAN broadcast. Reproduced by permission of Joseph Cirincione.

I love America.

Italy is a beautiful country, but I'm glad my grandparents came here 100 years ago. I truly believe America is one of the best countries the world has ever known. That is why it is so tragic what the policies of this administration [of George W. Bush] have done to the image and reputation of United States of America.

Seventeen months ago [September 2001], there were demonstrations around the world in support of the United States in the wake of [the terrorist attacks of] September 11 [2001]. Thousands of people gathered in hundreds of cities to express their support for the US. There were one million people in the streets of Tehran—in favor of the US. It is appalling how quickly this administration has squandered this support and sympathy for the United States.

I would like to quote *The Matrix*. One of my favorite scenes in the movie, is when Morpheus, played by Laurence Fishburne, is trying to teach Neo, played by Keanu Reeves, not just how to fight Kung-fu, but how to understand that the reality that he sees, feels and touches, is a false reality. It is a computer-generated virtual reality. Morpheus gives Neo a kick that sends him flying, and he wins their first match. He goes over to Neo and asks, "How did I beat you?" Neo replies, "You were faster than me," "Really?" says Morpheus, "Do you think my muscles had anything to do with my speed, here, in this world? Do you think that's air that you're breathing?" Keanu Reeves starts to get it. He gives that puzzled look—the only look he really has—and he starts to understand that the reality he knows is not true.

False Reality

I am not saying that the people in the White House are evil machines out to take over the world. However, they have constructed a false reality for us, a reality that we have bought into. Maybe not the people in this room, but we as a country. It is a reality where war equals peace. Invasion equals liberation. Military rule equals democracy. And [Iraqi leader] Saddam Hussein equals [terrorist] Osama bin Laden.

Half the people in this country think that Hussein was directly responsible for [the terrorist attack on the United States on] September 11 [2001]. There is not a shred of evidence that that is true. But it was a critical part of the campaign to convince us that it was urgent to take action. They had to convince America that Saddam was a terrorist, that Saddam has operational links to [bin Laden's terrorist group] al Qaeda. No serious intelligence analyst believes that to be the case, but the President has repeated it over and over. Like "Drink Coca-Cola." Iraq equals al Qaeda. Until now half of the American public believe it to be true. We're thirsty—we reach for a Coke. We want to strike back at al Qaeda, so we strike Iraq. This is a false reality. But only a part of the false reality.

The Iraq War Is Unreasonable

The war on Iraq is not reasonable since there is absolutely no evidence of an "imminent" threat to the US from Iraq or any evidence that Saddam [Hussein] will now use WMD [weapons of mass destruction]. Although [President George W.] Bush asserts that Saddam poses a "serious threat" to America, the "evidence" is to the contrary. Few doubt that Saddam has WMD, but, many question his willingness to use them against the US or anyone else and for good reason—the evidence that he will not is "compelling." Although Bush is attempting to create his own smokescreen for war, willingness to use WMD, is a central question to a war on Iraq.

D. Lindley Young, *The Modern Tribune*, January 25, 2003.
www.themoderntribune.com.

You have heard a great deal of talk of weapons of mass destruction [WMD]. What you may not realize is that this administration has now overturned fifty years of American policy and strategy on weapons of mass destruction. For fifty years the policy has been to eliminate the nuclear, chemical and biological weapons. The belief has been that as long as these weapons exist, someone is going to use them. This is why President [John F.] Kennedy warned in 1960 that if we did not do something, 15, 20 or 25 countries would have nuclear weapons by the end of that decade. But Kennedy did something. He started negotiating a treaty—the Nuclear Non-Proliferation Treaty. He couldn't finish the job; Lyndon Johnson did and Richard Nixon signed the treaty. Democrats and Republicans working together, side by side, with a bi-partisan consensus to eliminate these weapons.

That treaty has worked. There are still too many weapons; there are still too many countries, but instead of 15 or 25 countries, now we have eight. There are fewer nuclear weapons in the world now than there were ten years ago. There are fewer countries with WMD programs than there were ten years ago. We are making progress. This is also why Richard Nixon in 1969 [unilaterally] destroyed all of our biological weapons. *We* had the best biological weapons in the world. We had enough toxins to kill every man, woman and child and most food crops in the world. Nixon decided that this was not in our best national security interest. He negotiated the Biological Weapons Convention—which most countries in the world have now signed—to ban these evil weapons. So that no one would have them, no way, no time, no how.

Chemical Weapons Had to Be Destroyed

George H.W. Bush agreed. In 1991 he adopted the strategy that weapons had to be eliminated. He negotiated the Chemical Weapons Convention. When I was in the House of Representatives and working on the staff of the Armed Services Committee, we had debates in the late 1980s on an Army plan to build a new chemical weapon—a binary bomb. It would combine two chemicals in flight, forming a poison gas that would kill enemy troops. We had to have it, the Army said. Soldiers would die, if we did not deploy it. It was vital to US national security. But by 1991, George Bush was saying no one should have chemical weapons. We have now begun to destroy our 30,000 tons of chemical weapons. The Russians are destroying their 40,000 tons of chemical weapons. Over 145 countries have signed this treaty, which states that no one should have chemical weapons, nowhere, no how, no time. These are evil weapons and have no place in our world.

That was the strategy, a bipartisan strategy: focus on the proliferation of mass destruction weapons. President George [W.] Bush has now changed our strategy. In his recent State of the Union Address he amended the formula. Now, the danger is weapons of mass destruction *in the hands of outlaw regimes*. We have shifted from eliminating *weapons* to eliminating *regimes*. It is a strategy of picking and choosing. It's okay that Israel has 100 nuclear weapons—it's not okay that Iraq has nuclear weapons. It's okay that India has nuclear weapons—it's not okay that North Korea has nuclear weapons. It's okay that we have nuclear weapons—it's not okay that Iran does. It's a strategy of good guys and bad guys, a double standard.

This is a deeply flawed policy; it cannot be sustained. One reason is that the good guys and bad guys keep changing. Saddam Hussein is a monster. Did you hear anyone here support him? Do we have any appeasers here in this room? Did you hear anyone say that Saddam should stay in power? The world will be far better off when Saddam is gone, when his brutal regime passes into history. We all want to see him go.

The United States Kept Saddam in Power

He's been a monster for 30 years. The reason he stayed in power for so long is because he used to be *our* monster. We put [his] Baath Party in power. The CIA [Central Intelligence Agency] supported the coup that overthrew the pro-Soviet ruler of Iraq, General Abdel Karim Kassem, and brought the Baathists to power in 1963. Our CIA operatives liked the cut of Saddam's jib. We encouraged his rise when he became vice-president. When he took over as president in 1979, we didn't say a word when he liquidated the core of his own party's leadership. *We* sold him the chemicals that he used to build his chemical weapons. *We* sold him the biological agents that he used to build his biological weapons.

Did he build them? Absolutely. Was it a crime against humanity? Absolutely. Was it a crime that he killed 50,000 Iranians with chemical attacks in the Iran-Iraq War? Yes. Did the Reagan Administration do anything to stop it? No, we did not. We wanted to kill Iranians, and Saddam was doing just that. We sent [secretary of state] Donald Rumsfeld to seal the deal in 1983 and again in 1984 (during Iraq's chemical attacks on Iranian troops), to restore relations with Saddam's regime and make sure that Saddam and the US were in close coordination on policy. Did those good relations help us stop him when he gassed 10,000 Kurds in Halabja in 1988? They did not. We did not even try. We had sold him the helicopters he used to spray the poison gas.

We kept him in power. Now he has changed, now he's evil and has to go. I believe he has to go. But that is the problem with the good guy/bad guy strategy. Now, we want democracy in Iran. Iran use to have a democracy—*we* overthrew it in 1954. We put the Shah of Iran in power. We supported that evil dictatorship and kept him in power. We sold the Shah his first nuclear reactor. When the people in Iran did then what some say they should do now, when they rose up and overthrew the dictatorship, we did not like the results and we have been campaigning against the new Iranian government ever since. Is it an undemocratic government? Yes. Would I like to see us invade Iran next? No. Yet some people in this administration are in favor of invading Iran. That is the next country on their "To Do" list.

The reason there is no exit strategy for Iraq [after the 2003 war] is because some of these guys do not want to leave. Remember the Powell Doctrine? One, use overwhelming force—we may have that. Two, clear political objectives—sorry, do not see that. Three, support of the American people—well, today, maybe, but it has been up and down all year [in 2003]. Fourth and finally, there is no exit strategy. You need to understand that Iraq is a part of a grander strategy. This is not about WMD, it's not about terrorism. It's about seeing that the US, the most powerful nation that the world has ever known, uses its power to transform the world.

Starting a "Democratic Tsunami"

Some people are advocating this with noble intentions. They want to do good in the world, but they want to do it through the use of military power. They want to start with Iraq, and then they believe that Iraq will let off a "democratic tsunami" in the region. They believe that with US help we can topple the government of Syria, breaking the Syrian grip on Lebanon, eliminating the operating bases for [the terrorist groups] Hamas and Hezbollah, and thus improving the security situation for Israel. In this process we will transform the Palestinian Authority into a democratic organization, giving the Israelis a reliable negotiation partner for a final peace settlement. The reason this president has not spent more than two hours on Middle East peace is that for him the road to Jerusalem goes through Baghdad. We will also deal with our problem in Saudi Arabia by moving the bases from Saudi Arabia to Iraq. We will establish a pro-American regime that can host our troops and consolidate a permanent American presence in the Gulf.

You think that I am making this up?

Go read the *2002 National Security Strategy for the United States*, which holds that our defense "will require bases and stations within and beyond Western Europe and Northeast Asia." Or come to Carnegie Non-Proliferation web site. You can find on our site all the documents arguing for this strategy going back ten years. Read the 2000 report from the neo-conservative Project for the New American Century signed by many current administration officials. The report says, "The U.S. has for decades sought to play a more permanent role in the Gulf regional security. While the unresolved conflict with Iraq provides the immediate justification, the need for a substantial American force presence in the Gulf transcends the issue of the regime of Saddam Hussein."

When did the planning of this war begin? It began the day President [George H.W.] Bush stopped the 1991 war. There were some people in that Administration that never wanted to stop. [Deputy Secretary of Defense] Paul Wolfowitz sat in the corner in a huff, according to reporters. He never wanted to stop the war. Neo-conservatives thought that we had not finished the job; they wanted us to begin the war again. So they planned and organized. They started with the Wolfowitz draft *Defense Policy Guidelines* in 1992. There, he talked about establishing the permanent supremacy of US power in the world. No one should be allowed to challenge our power, he wrote. Not regionally, not globally. He advocated adopting a policy of pre-emption. He wrote of being prepared for a war with Iraq—in 1992. When that plan was leaked to the *New York Times*, (thank god for leakers) it was considered so outrageous, so extreme, they were forced to withdraw the draft and rewrite it. "Pre-emption" was replaced with "containment."

They thought they would get another try with the strategy plans next year, but the American people voted them out of power. Some guy from Arkansas became president [Bill Clinton], and they were furious. They spent their years in exile well. They learned, studied and organized, and now as a group they have entered the government and have key positions in the State Department and in the Defense Department, and now have a hammerlock on the national security policy apparatus of the US. For them, Iraq is just the beginning. As one of the officials said to me "we have a long 'to do' list."

We have failed to stop this war [in Iraq]. It is an unnecessary war. [Weapons] inspections could have worked; they could have done the job. It was not necessary to go to war at this time, in this place with a Potemkin coalition[1] with no international organization behind us. But that does not mean we have failed. This battle is just beginning.

If you're a student, this is a wonderful time to be a student. Before you the most important political experiment of our time is being conducted. Study it, learn from it, organize around it.

And make sure that this never happens again.

1. a sham coalition designed to hide the fact that the United States had no international backing

Periodical Bibliography

The following articles have been selected to supplement the diverse views presented in this chapter.

Marjorie Cohn — "Invading Iraq Would Compound the Terror," *Jurist*, April 5, 2002. www.jurist.law.pitt.edu.

Jonathon Gatehouse — "The New World Order," *Maclean's*, January 27, 2003.

Reuel Marc Gerecht — "A Necessary War: Unless Saddam Hussein Is Removed, the War on Terror Will Fail," *Weekly Standard*, October 21, 2002. www.weeklystandard.com.

Thom Hartmann — "The Crime of the Century: A Never-Ending War Against Terrorism," *Common Dreams News Center*, April 30, 2003. www.commondreams.org.

Chalmers Johnson — "Responding to Terrorism Without Committing Terrorism," *Los Angeles Times*, September 30, 2001.

David E. Kaplan et al. — "Playing Offense," *U.S. News & World Report*, June 2, 2003.

Michael T. Klare — "What Kind of War?" *AlterNet*, September 17, 2001. www.alternet.org.

Nicholas Lemann — "Real Reasons," *New Yorker*, September 22, 2003.

Raymond Lotta — "U.S. Imperialism's Crusade for One Empire," *Revolutionary Worker*, February 16, 2003.

Michael Meacher — "This War on Terrorism Is Bogus," *Guardian*, September 6, 2003. www.commondreams.org.

Dan Morgan and David B. Ottaway — "In Iraq War Scenario, Oil Is Key Issue," *Washington Post*, September 15, 2002. www.washingtonpost.com.

Paul Rogers — "Oil and the War on Terrorism: Why Is the United States in the Gulf?" *openDemocracy*, September 1, 2002. www.opendemocracy.com.

Lance Selfa — "Getting the War They Wanted," *Socialist Worker*, February 14, 2003. www.socialistworker.org.

Ken Silverstein — "No War for Oil," *American Prospect*, August 12, 2002. www.prospect.org.

Joe Sobran — "What Happened to the War on Terrorism?" *SOBRAN'S*, February 6, 2003. www.sobran.com.

CHAPTER 2

Is the Domestic War on Terrorism a Threat to Civil Liberties?

Chapter Preface

Two months after the September 11, 2001, terrorist attacks on the United States, President George W. Bush authorized military tribunals to conduct trials involving non-U.S. citizens accused of terrorism. Bush's tribunal authorization, issued as an emergency executive order not requiring congressional approval, was the first action of its kind since World War II. In 1942 then-president Theodore Roosevelt ordered eight captured Nazis—saboteurs who sneaked into the United States allegedly to blow up military and civilian installations—tried by secret military court. Six of the eight Nazis were sentenced to death. Many legal and political experts and human rights activists argue that the secrecy of military tribunals and the lack of constitutional protections for the accused threaten civil liberties.

According to Laura W. Murphy, director of the national office of the American Civil Liberties Union,

> The use of military tribunals would apparently authorize secret trials without a jury and without the requirement of a unanimous verdict and would limit a defendant's opportunities to confront the evidence against him and choose his own lawyer. What's worse, these important legal protections would be removed in a situation where defendants may very well be facing the death penalty.

Proponents of the use of military tribunals to try terrorist suspects, however, claim that these suspects are not entitled to the same rights as the U.S. citizens they are accused of attacking. Vice President Dick Cheney says, "They don't deserve the same guarantees and safeguards that we use for an American citizen. They will have a fair trial under the procedures of the military tribunal." Moreover, Attorney General John Ashcroft argues that trying terrorists in civilian courts could result in inadvertent leaking of defense secrets. "War criminals have always been tried in military courts," he claims.

The use of military tribunals to try suspected terrorists continues to be hotly debated. Authors in the following chapters discuss expanded law enforcement powers, racial profiling, and the detention of immigrants as they explore how the war on terrorism affects civil liberties.

"Essentially, though, with the USA PATRIOT Act they have cracked down on personal liberty without providing greater security."

The USA PATRIOT Act Threatens Civil Liberties

Kelly Patricia O'Meara

The USA PATRIOT Act, passed in response to the September 11, 2001, terrorist attacks, expands law enforcements powers. In the following viewpoint Kelly Patricia O'Meara argues that the act sacrifices civil liberties in the name of national security but does little to help the war on terrorism. Curtailing individual liberties, she insists, is a victory for the terrorists. O'Meara maintains that both conservative and liberal civil libertarians oppose the USA PATRIOT Act on the grounds that it violates the First, Fourth, Fifth, Sixth, Eighth, and Thirteenth Amendments to the Constitution. Moreover, she insists that the majority of the people impacted by the act are not terrorists. Kelly Patricia O'Meara is an investigative reporter for *Insight on the News*.

As you read, consider the following questions:

1. In the author's opinion, what do critics say is the main problem with the USA PATRIOT Act?
2. According to O'Meara, what are "Sneak and Peek" warrants?
3. What does the author argue was the reason that the Department of Justice scaled back the TIPS program?

Kelly Patricia O'Meara, "Losing the War for Civil Liberties; Civil Libertarians Contend Politicians Have Pulled a Bait and Switch by Using the War on Terrorism to Implement Intrusive—and Unconstitutional—Security Measures," *Insight on the News*, vol. 18, September 16, 2002, pp. 18–20.

It used to be that Americans packed for air travel with a mental checklist of personal items needed for their holiday or business engagement: which clothes to bring, shoes, cameras, etc. Today, however, in the backwash of the Sept. 11, [2001 terrorist] attacks on the U.S. mainland, a new and more detailed (often ridiculous) list of concerns must be considered.

No eyebrow tweezers, for instance, no fingernail files or clippers, no toothpicks, no rat-tail combs, no letter openers or anything that even resembles a knife, and just two (count 'em, two) throw-away lighters. Every one of these items, apparently, is considered a security threat and, if noticed by the new federal airport-security force, will land a passenger at the end of the conveyer belt for a public shakedown and perhaps worse.

While time-consuming, embarrassing, annoying and sometimes frightening, the new airline-security measures pale in comparison to a number of other (more invasive) provisions federal lawmakers authorized in the immediate aftermath of the terrorist attacks on the World Trade Center and the Pentagon. Civil libertarians charge that the new security measures sacrifice political freedom in the name of national security while contributing little or nothing to the war on terror.

New Government Powers Threaten America's Freedom

Either way, the terrorists win. A little more than one month after the Sept. 11 terrorist attacks, public enemy No. 1 [September 11 mastermind] Osama bin Laden, predicted that "freedom and human rights in America are doomed. The U.S. government will lead the American people—and the West in general—into an unbearable hell and a choking life." During the year following the bin Laden attacks, sweeping new government powers indeed have been authorized that civil libertarians say threaten the freedoms Americans are told this nation's enemies hate.

Many of these powers were authorized in a flush of panic by the Uniting and Strengthening America by Providing Appropriate Tools Required to Intercept and Obstruct Terrorism Act, or USA PATRIOT Act. Passed before members of Congress even could read it, this law provides sweeping powers to state and federal law-enforcement officials to combat terrorism. The problem, critics say, is that under these new powers every American citizen is a possible suspect of terrorism. On the right, *Insight* is on record as opposing this law from the moment of its passage. On the left, the American Civil Liberties Union (ACLU) has worked tirelessly to resist assaults on civil liberties arising from the Sept. 11 attacks and has focused on the act.

Indeed, ACLU Executive Director Anthony Romero tells *Insight* "We've been enormously concerned that the war on terrorism has fundamentally eroded civil liberties in the country. You have a system of checks and balances that has been upset by Attorney General John Ashcroft; you have actions taken by the Justice Department that have been veiled in a cloak of secrecy; and you have wholesale abridgement of the Bill of Rights even in cases involving American citizens. All of our efforts have been focused on the effort to keep in place a system of checks and balances."

What Is Wrong with the Act?

The ACLU has been relentless in publicizing what its leaders say they regard as the most egregious of the new security measures under the USA PATRIOT Act, including but not limited to the following:

• The law allows for indefinite detention of noncitizens who are not terrorists on minor visa violations.

• It minimizes judicial supervision of telephone and Internet surveillance by law-enforcement authorities in antiterrorism investigations and in routine criminal investigations unrelated to terrorism.

• The act expands the ability of the government to conduct secret searches—even in criminal investigations unrelated to terrorism.

• It gives the attorney general and the secretary of state the power to designate domestic groups as terrorist organizations.

• The new law grants the FBI broad access to sensitive medical, financial, mental-health and educational records about individuals without having to show evidence of a crime and without a court order.

• The act allows searches of highly personal financial records without notice and without judicial review, based on a very low standard that does not require the showing of probable cause of a crime or even relevance to an ongoing terrorism investigation.

• It creates a broad new definition of "domestic terrorism" that could allow a police sweep of people who engage in acts of public protest and subject them to wiretapping and enhanced penalties.

• And this law allows the sharing of sensitive information in criminal cases with intelligence agencies, including the CIA, National Security Agency, Immigration and Naturalization Service and the Secret Service.

Englehart. © 1997 by Bob Englehart. Reproduced by permission.

"The searches and seizures that have us the most concerned," continues Romero, "are the 'Sneak and Peek' warrants that allow the government to come into a citizen's home and search their personal effects, take photographs, download information off their computers and not inform them of the search until after the fact. The problem with this is that sometimes law enforcement gets it wrong. They may have the wrong name, the wrong address, or the judge might have signed the wrong warrant."

What Went Wrong

According to Romero, "The problem is that we haven't asked the most basic threshold question that we needed to ask before we started adding all the law-enforcement intelligence powers—how did Sept. 11 happen? Were law enforcement and intelligence officials using their extensive powers to their fullest extent prior to Sept. 11 and, if not, why not? We need to know what broke down before we can figure out the remedy. Unfortunately, Congress didn't address those issues. It's only now that they're looking at those issues."

The ACLU executive director adds: "Americans don't fully realize what has happened to some core American principles and basic workings of our democracy. Most Americans don't realize that American citizens are being held on American soil without access to lawyers and no charges having been brought against them. This fundamentally puts the Bill of Rights on its head—there's no such thing anymore as the presumption of being innocent until proved guilty. This is just fundamentally un-American."

Civil libertarians, both on the left and the right, insist that the USA PATRIOT Act violates the First Amendment guarantee of freedom of speech; the Fourth Amendment prohibition of unreasonable searches and seizures; the Fifth Amendment right to due process; the Sixth Amendment guarantees of speedy and fair trial; the Eighth Amendment prohibition of cruel and unusual punishment; and the 13th Amendment prohibition against punishment by servitude without conviction.

The Act Impacts Innocent People

John Whitehead, founder and president of the Rutherford Institute, a leading advocate of civil liberties and human rights, tells *Insight* that "the problem with a lot of the USA PATRIOT Act and some of the presidential Executive Orders is that the 99.9 percent of the people in this country who are not terrorists will be impacted by these laws. How can you suddenly introduce broadly encompassing laws which allow the government to search your e-mails, check your library books, do 'Sneak and Peek' searches of your home, turn your neighbor into a spy through the TIPS [Terrorist Information and Prevention System] program, etc., without hearings or so much as asking how these laws will stop terrorism?"

Whitehead says that, if this law stands, "The Fourth Amendment will have been totally blown. What the Fourth Amendment says is that you have to individualize suspicion, a judge has to carefully look at it and it has to be reasonable. Today, everything is considered suspicious." But, says Whitehead, "I'm hopeful that we'll look back in 10 years and say this was all crazy stuff. Back in the 1940s we put Japanese-Americans in prison camps, in the 1950s we had the McCarthy era [during which people thought to be Communists were harrassed] and in the 1960s there was government harassment of the hippies and [civil rights leader] Martin Luther King. Today, most of us look back and say all that was wrong, so there is hope."

According to Whitehead, "Freedom and security are not mutually exclusive, but the only thing between us and tyranny is the Constitution of the United States. Do I think we've lost civil liberties? Yes. Have we set the groundwork for a police state? Yes. The question is whether we can reverse it. To do so will take a courageous administration led by a president of great intellect—and a Congress that not only reads the bills it passes but which looks carefully at legislation and compares it with the clear meaning of the Constitution rather than the direction of the latest opinion polls."

The TIPS program to which Whitehead referred was created by the Department of Justice (DOJ) as a "national information-sharing system" which enlists the support of workers in the community to report "suspicious" activity to the government. Neighborhood groups also were recruited as in Cuba to report on "unfamiliar" people in the community or those whose behavior is "suspicious" or "not normal." The tipsters were to include the local cable guy, trash collectors and others. But the idea of assigning neighbor to watch neighbor finally raised such a flap that the DOJ scaled back its snoop network to limit the hot-line tattletales to workers involved in the "transportation, trucking, shipping, maritime and mass-transit industries."

The United States Is Closer to a Police State

Dave Kopel, research director for the Independence Institute, a nonprofit policy-research organization, tells *Insight* that "the misnamed USA PATRIOT Act has plenty of search-and-seizure provisions that are not limited to terrorism even under the new, very broad definition. These would allow secret searches of your house—warrantless searches without regard to whether it's a terrorism offense." Kopel says, "The FBI with the active assistance of the DOJ and White House pulled a real bait and switch on the American people. They said we've got to have these emergency powers for fighting terrorism, and what they really got was a whole lot of non-emergency powers for nonterrorist purposes. It's not a police state yet, but we're closer to it, and there has to be continued vigilance among the people. TIPS has received a lot of negative public reaction and they've scaled it back some. But the problem with the USA PATRIOT Act is that it has little to do with fighting terrorism."

According to Kopel, "We're safer from terrorists because we've bombed the hell out of [the terrorist group] al-Qaeda and the Taliban [in Afghanistan, which was harboring it], but that didn't have anything to do with these new laws. We had the ability to do that before the new legislation. Today we have a much higher level of intrusiveness without greater security. It would be one thing to change your birthright of liberty for greater security—at least you're making that trade-off. Essentially, though, with the USA PATRIOT Act they have cracked down on personal liberty without providing greater security."

Rep. Ron Paul (R-Texas), a libertarian who is one of only three Republican lawmakers to have voted against the USA PATRIOT Act, and an outspoken critic, tells *Insight:* "The so-called PATRIOT Act condones and institutionalizes everything and has really opened up a Pandora's box." He says, "I think there is a strong determination on the part of government to know everything about everybody, and fighting terrorism is the excuse, not the reason. All of these laws have been in the mill for years, and everything now is in place for what some people describe as a police state. I think we're on the verge of a very, very tough police state in this country—and it will only end when Americans are fed up. So far people are terrified to say anything. Hopefully, we'll wake up before it's too late."

"According to a recent poll, 91 percent of the public says that the [Patriot Act] hasn't affected their own civil liberties."

The USA PATRIOT Act Does Not Threaten Civil Liberties

Kate O'Beirne

The USA PATRIOT Act, which grants law enforcement expanded powers, was passed in the aftermath of the September 11, 2001, terrorist attacks. The PATRIOT Act preserves civil liberties while preventing further terrorist attacks on the United States, Kate O'Beirne argues in the following viewpoint. She maintains that lawmakers' ignorance of the act combined with disinformation spread by the American Civil Liberties Union, hostile media reports, and an overreaction from Democratic presidential hopefuls have led to the mistaken notion that the PATRIOT Act is a threat to civil liberties. O'Beirne insists that over 90 percent of Americans do not believe that the PATRIOT Act has infringed upon their civil liberties. Kate O'Beirne is an attorney and the Washington editor of the *National Review*.

As you read, consider the following questions:
1. According to the author, in what three ways has the ability of federal law enforcement been updated to fight the threat of terrorism?
2. How often is the Justice Department required to provide Congress with details on the implementation of the Patriot Act, according to O'Beirne?

Kate O'Beirne, "Congress's Patriotic Act: This Is a Law That Defends America and, Yes, Preserves Civil Liberties, Dammit," www.nationalreview.com, September 15, 2003. Copyright © 2003 by National Review, Inc. Reproduced by permission of United Feature Syndicate, Inc.

Who says you can't argue with success? In the past two years [2001–2003], terrorist cells in Buffalo, Detroit, Seattle, and Portland, Ore., have been dismantled; criminal charges have been brought against 225 suspected terrorists; and 132 of those suspects have been convicted. Terrorists haven't carried out another attack here because the domestic war on terrorism, aimed at prevention, has worked. Yet in July [2003], 113 Republicans voted with a large House majority against a provision in the USA Patriot Act that federal officials see as playing a crucial role in disrupting terrorist plots. Lawmakers' ignorance of the law, the ACLU's [American Civil Liberties Union] effective disinformation campaign, a hostile media, and hysterical, partisan attacks from the presidential campaign trail now have the administration playing defense, despite its remarkably successful offense against terrorism.

Prompted by the recent vote, Attorney General John Ashcroft has embarked on a tour of 18 cities to make the case for the Patriot Act to the public. Ashcroft reminds his audiences that the law, passed in the Senate by a 98-to-1 vote (and in the House by 357 to 66) six weeks after the September 11 [2001 terrorist] attacks, updated the ability of federal law enforcement to confront the threat of terrorism in three central ways. It removed the legal barriers that prevented law enforcement and intelligence agencies from sharing information and coordinating activities—barriers that Congress criticized in its report on what went wrong before 9/11. It brought surveillance laws from the era of the rotary phone into the age of cell phones and Internet communications. And it extended the authority that federal investigators use against the mafia and drug dealers to cover terrorists.

Where Congress overwhelmingly saw commonsense provisions clearly justified to protect American lives, hysterical critics are seeing a power grab by a would-be totalitarian state. According to a *Los Angeles Times* story, the Patriot Act amounts to "the legislative equivalent of a blank check." The *Cleveland Plain Dealer* spots the "seedstock of a police state." In an alarming *Newsday* op-ed, Sam Dash, the former chief counsel to the Senate Watergate Committee, warns of a presidential abuse of power that rivals the "horror" committed by

Richard Nixon. Dash is now a law professor at Georgetown—but, like most of the Patriot Act alarmists, he doesn't cite a single provision of the objectionable law to bolster his case.

Nonspecific Criticisms Abound

Democratic presidential candidates are no more specific. In his "first five seconds as president," Dick Gephardt would fire Ashcroft. Sen. [John] Edwards gets standing ovations for declaring, "We cannot allow people like John Ashcroft to take away our rights and our freedoms." John Kerry vows that when he's president, "there will be no John Ashcroft trampling on the Bill of Rights." Each one of them voted for the Patriot Act; but Howard Dean, a former governor, routinely assails the law itself for eroding "the rights of average Americans," and calls for its repeal.

A Key Weapon in the Fight Against Terrorism

Congress overwhelmingly approved the USA PATRIOT Act. In the House, Representatives voted 357 to 66 for the measure, while the Senate supported the legislation by a near unanimous 98-to-1 vote.

The PATRIOT Act gave us the tools we needed to integrate our law enforcement and intelligence capabilities to win the war on terror.

It allowed the Department of Justice to use the same tools from the criminal process on terrorists that we use to combat mobsters or drug dealers. We use these tools to gather intelligence and to prevent terrorists from unleashing more death and destruction within our country. We use these tools to connect the "dots." We use these tools to save innocent lives. . . .

Let me state this as clearly as possible.

Our ability to prevent another catastrophic attack on American soil would be more difficult, if not impossible, without the PATRIOT Act. It has been the key weapon used across America in successful counter-terrorist operations to protect innocent Americans from the deadly plans of terrorists.

Testimony of Attorney General John Ashcroft before the U.S. House of Representatives Committee on the Judiciary, June 5, 2003.

Even when the media criticize a specific part of the new law, they usually get it wrong. In May [2003], a major *Time* magazine story was subtitled, "Can Attorney General John

Ashcroft fight terrorism on our shores without injuring our freedoms?" The demonstrable answer is yes. But the article was riddled with mistakes that led to a different conclusion. For example, the authors asserted, "If you are suspected of terrorist links, law enforcement can access your records, conduct wiretaps and electronic surveillance, search and seize private property and make secret arrests—all without a warrant." In fact, federal authorities can't do any of those things without obtaining a court order.

In July [2003], when Reps. C.L. "Butch" Otter (R., Idaho) and Dennis Kucinich (D., Ohio) argued for their amendment to prohibit funding for delayed-notification warrants, the discussion on the House floor was equally ignorant. If lawmakers don't want to be bothered understanding the law, they could at least try watching [the TV show] *The Sopranos* to learn how federal investigators lawfully operate. Section 213, the Patriot Act provision that the Otter amendment would de-fund, allows federal investigators to ask a court for permission to temporarily delay notifying a suspect that a court-issued search warrant has been executed. Sens. Patrick Leahy (D., Vt.) and Orrin Hatch (R., Utah) sponsored the provision, which permits delayed notification when there is a risk of flight, injury to an individual, intimidation of witnesses, destruction of evidence, or the serious jeopardizing of an investigation. In 1979, the Supreme Court called an argument that the practice is unconstitutional "frivolous." Without the ability to postpone notice of a warrant, investigators would be unable to install a wiretap in a terrorist's apartment without first informing the suspect.

Only 47 Delayed-Notice Warrants Were Issued

The Justice Department is required to provide Congress with details on the implementation of the Patriot Act twice a year. In a 60-page report this May [2003], the department explained that in the past two years, delayed-notice warrants under Section 213 had been sought (and approved) by courts just 47 times. This wasn't mentioned during the House's hasty consideration of the Otter amendment. Instead, Rep. Otter ludicrously claimed that Section 213 permits the CIA to operate domestically. Rep. Kucinich ignored the federal courts that have upheld the constitutionality of delaying notification of a warrant, and rested his own constitutional objection on the "common law." The amendment has not yet passed the Senate, but the administration is threatening a veto if it does. [The amendment did not pass.]

A Republican congressional aide explains that over 100 House Republicans were not so much relying on Dennis Kucinich's legal opinions as they were reflecting what they are hearing from their constituents back home. The aide reports that his office is receiving copies of news articles about the Patriot Act from Republican constituents concerned about the alleged assaults on civil liberties. Another GOP aide notes that constituents vehemently opposed to the war in Iraq also strenuously object to the Patriot Act; voting for the amendment "gives members some cover."

Former assistant attorney general Viet Dinh, who began crafting the Patriot Act within days of 9/11, has been publicly engaging its critics over their wildly exaggerated case. In a recent debate, when Dinh had successfully defended the act's provisions, his opponent finally allowed that the alarming problem "is not within the Patriot Act, but the milieu of fear you've created." That would be a small milieu. According to a recent poll, 91 percent of the public says that the act hasn't affected their own civil liberties.

Critics of the Patriot Act would rather rely on hypothetical questions, such as that cited recently in *USA Today*. According to Gallup, only 33 percent of Americans favor the government's taking all steps necessary to prevent terrorism "even if it means that your basic civil liberties would be violated." The two-thirds that would oppose eroding civil liberties includes Attorney General John Ashcroft.

"Racial profiling is racial discrimination—clear and simple. If you still doubt that fact, then consider why racial profiling is never proposed in the case of white criminals."

Racial Profiling Is a Threat to Civil Liberties

Peter G. Simonson

Racial profiling for the purpose of identifying terrorists is discriminatory and therefore a violation of civil liberties, Peter G. Simonson argues in the following viewpoint. He maintains that racial profiling should never be considered a legitimate instrument in the war on terrorism because the concept of race is completely arbitrary. He warns that once Congress legalizes racial profiling to fight terrorism, race-based traffic stops and drug searches will also became permissible. Any gains racial profiling might provide in the war on terrorism would be offset by the consequent loss of civil liberties, Simonson insists. Peter G. Simonson is executive director of the American Civil Liberties Union of New Mexico.

As you read, consider the following questions:
1. In the author's opinion, racial profiling hinges on what simple stereotypes?
2. According to Simonson, why is racial profiling never proposed in the case of white criminals?
3. Why does the author argue that racial profiling is unnecessary?

It's a bad sign for civil rights when two well-known essayists from opposite sides of the political spectrum agree that racial profiling is a rational tool to prevent terrorism. In recent weeks, columns by both William F. Buckley and Michael Kinsley were published in the [*Albuquerque*] *Journal* arguing that airport security officials should single out "Arab-looking men" for "intrusive inspections." Kinsley even concludes that the only cost of racial profiling to minorities is "pretty small: inconvenience and embarrassment."

That's a pretty bold statement coming from a white man of some stature and privilege—a man who will never live the experience of a Chicana friend of mine, for example, who was in New York City during the [September 11, 2001, terrorist] attack. As she awaited her flight back to Albuquerque in a bar at Kennedy airport, a television flashed nighttime scenes of the Afghan opposition bombing the Taliban's stronghold in Kabul.[1] Thinking that the U.S. was behind the attack, people in the bar raucously cheered to see flames rising from the city. At that point my friend noted that she was the only woman of color in a room full of revved-up white men in various states of intoxication.

"Were they going to think that I was from Afghanistan, that I was a terrorist?" she asked herself. Fear of that possibility, and what people might do as a result, drove her from the bar and nagged at her for the remainder of the trip.

A key reason why racial profiling should never be considered a legitimate tool for law enforcement is that the concept of race is absolutely arbitrary. Who among us can distinguish an Afghan or a Saudi man from a crowd of people as diverse as that which passes through most East Coast airports? It is to be hoped that we've all learned enough from the . . . murder of Balbir Singh Sodhi, a Sikh gas station owner in Mesa, Ariz., to know that a beard and a turban do not a terrorist make.

Unavoidably, racial profiling hinges on simple stereotypes of what certain ethnic and religious groups look like, how they speak, and how their last names sound. Those facile

---

1. The Taliban, Afghanistan's ruling party, was accused by the Bush administration of harboring the terrorists responsible for the September 11 attacks.

categories quickly shatter against the hard reality of ethnic diversity, and when they do, profiling becomes a free-for-all to scrutinize any person of color. And innocent people are unlawfully searched, detained, and sometimes jailed.

Should the U.S. Detain Immigrant Men from Some Countries for Visa Violations?

No, unfairly targets Arabs and Muslims

15%

Yes, enforce immigration law

49%

Not unless there's evidence they're terrorists

4%

Yes, but why didn't INS show them the door sooner?

32%

Total Votes: 1277

San Francisco Chronicle, January 11, 2003.

Racial profiling is racial discrimination—clear and simple. If you still doubt that fact, then consider why racial profiling is never proposed in the case of white criminals. Where was the clamor for federal courthouses to "intrusively inspect" thin, white men with crew cuts [who look like bomber Timothy McVeigh] after the Oklahoma City bombing? I fear the notion never came up because people in positions of power assume, unconsciously or otherwise, that "whiteness" is the standard against which other races are profiled.

Once law enforcement authorities demonstrate that it's OK to automatically suspect people of Islamic faith or Middle Eastern descent of terrorist inclinations, the public adopts that suspicion as well. As the recent wave of race-based crimes across the country has shown, that suspicion readily adds up to hate, and hate to violence.

Once Congress passes laws that make racial profiling OK for the specific purpose of combating terrorism, some attorney somewhere will twist the meaning of that law to justify race-based traffic stops or drug searches in other, non-terrorist contexts. From there, it's a slippery slope to the mentality that driving while black means you're just asking for trouble from the police.

Federal law enforcement already has far-reaching authority to find and neutralize any person remotely suspected of terrorist involvement—they just need to use it, and use it well. Americans should not stand to see that authority expanded to include racial profiling.

Whatever benefits we derive in the battle against terrorism will pale in comparison to the damage done to race relations in this country and constitutional guarantees of equal protection under law.

"Racial classifications are allowed if they are 'narrowly tailored' to a 'compelling governmental interest.'. . . If stopping terrorism is not a compelling interest, then nothing is."

Racial Profiling Is Not a Threat to Civil Liberties

Roger Clegg

In the following viewpoint Roger Clegg insists that scrutinizing Arab American airline passengers who fit a very specific terrorist profile is not a violation of civil liberties. He argues that the Supreme Court allows racial profiling that is narrowly focused and serves a compelling governmental interest, such as the prevention of terrorism. Roger Clegg is general counsel at the Center for Equal Opportunity, a conservative think tank devoted to the promotion of colorblind equal opportunity, and a contributing editor for *National Review Online*.

As you read, consider the following questions:

1. According to Clegg, why is specific-description profiling not properly considered racial profiling?
2. What is the classic case of racial profiling, in the author's opinion?
3. Why should people who look Middle Eastern be willing to endure racial profiling, according to the author?

Roger Clegg, "Profiling Terrorists: A Dose of Realism," www.nationalreview.com, September 18, 2001. Copyright © 2001 by National Review, Inc. Reproduced by permission of United Feature Syndicate, Inc.

A few news stories . . . have reported on the fear of some people that the government will use "racial profiling" in trying to identify terrorists. To which there are two responses. First, it is not at all clear that what will be used really is racial profiling. And, second, so what?

If you are mugged by a six-foot-two-inch, black male wearing a red sweatshirt, it is not "racial profiling" for the police to be on the lookout for people who meet that description, even though one element in it is racial. The classic case of racial profiling is, instead, when the police decide to stop cars being driven by young black males, not because they have the description of a specific suspect, but because they know that statistically drugs are more likely to be smuggled by young black males than, say, old Asian females.

But there are other circumstances that fall in between these two extremes. Suppose, for instance, that you are looking for members of a particular drug cartel, who are engaged in particular acts of smuggling, and you know that they will all be Colombian nationals, but you don't have specific names or descriptions that go beyond that. Is it "racial profiling" to look harder at dark-eyed, dark-haired, darker-skin whites, and give shorter shrift to Asians, blacks, and folks with blond or red hair?

Enough hypotheticals. Suppose that you have already identified several members of a terrorist ring and want to find the rest. The ones you have identified so far meet a particular profile: Middle Eastern descent. Moslem. Several are trained pilots. Male. Young or middle-aged. Booked on transcontinental flights. Any problem with assuming that there is a good chance that the remaining members of the ring are likely to meet this profile, too?

Intense Scrutiny Is Not Racial Profiling

This is a lot closer to the specific-description extreme of the spectrum than the statistically speaking end of the spectrum. Which means that this really isn't properly characterized as racial profiling at all. This doesn't mean you ignore everyone who doesn't meet the profile or shoot to kill anyone with black hair. But you look harder at those who fit the description.

But the other response is, so what if it *is* racial profiling? No one believes that the government should never, under any circumstances, consider race in its actions.

Racial Profiling Makes Flying Safer

The mathematical probability that a randomly chosen Arab passenger might attempt a mass-murder-suicide hijacking—while tiny—is considerably higher than the probability that a randomly chosen white, black, Hispanic, or Asian passenger might do the same. In constitutional-law parlance, while racial profiling may be presumptively unconstitutional, that presumption is overcome in the case of airline passengers, because the government has a compelling interest in preventing mass-murder-suicide hijackings, and because close scrutiny of Arab-looking people is narrowly tailored to protect that interest. . . .

Arab-Americans understandably resent being singled out for special scrutiny when boarding airliners. But the alternatives—a greater risk of being killed and greater political pressure for detention of relatives and other visitors from abroad who fall under unwarranted suspicion—are worse.

Stuart Taylor Jr., *The Atlantic Online*, www.theatlantic.com, September 25, 2001.

Suppose a prison has just suffered a race riot. Would it be barred from temporarily segregating prisoners? Of course not, as several of the justices noted—with none disagreeing—in one Supreme Court case. In an earlier decision, another justice wrote that the Constitution is not a suicide pact. Just so, and thus one would not expect it to bar the government from doing what is necessary to defend the ordered liberty of our society.

Racial classifications are allowed if they are "narrowly tailored" to a "compelling governmental interest," according to the Supreme Court's case law. If stopping terrorism is not a compelling interest, then nothing is. And in some circumstances there will be no way to safeguard this interest without taking the ethnicity of suspects into account. Such discrimination should be as limited and temporary as possible, but it is preferable to allowing mass murder, as all three branches of government would surely conclude.

And I doubt that few people would complain about it. My boss, a Latina, suspects that she is often assumed to be Middle Eastern when she travels on international flights, and that in Europe she is therefore more often stopped by security guards. She has no problem with that. And why should she—why should anyone—if the alternative is to diminish, however slightly, the chances of catching the next terrorist?

"Detention without evidence is not the hallmark of a free society."

Detaining Immigrants to Prevent Future Terrorist Attacks Violates Their Civil Liberties

Anita Ramasastry

Anita Ramasastry argues in the following viewpoint that the government's use of "preventive detention"—the imprisonment of immigrants without evidence of their involvement in terrorist activity in the hope of preventing future terrorist attacks—is a violation of civil liberties. She insists that after the September 11, 2001, terrorist attacks the FBI went too far in detaining aliens who may have violated immigration laws but who had no connection to terrorism. Moreover, many of those detained were verbally and physically abused while in custody. Anita Ramasastry is an assistant professor of law at the University of Washington School of Law in Seattle and the associate director of the Shidler Center for Law, Commerce, and Technology.

As you read, consider the following questions:
1. What is the Office of the Inspector General (OIG), according to the author?
2. In Ramasastry's opinion, what was the average length of time from arrest to clearance for immigrant detainees?
3. According to the author, how many of the 272 complaints about detention received by the Office of the Inspector General were deemed credible and investigated?

[In summer 2003] the Office of the Inspector General ("OIG") for the United States Department of Justice ("DOJ") issued two reports relating to the treatment of certain immigrant detainees after [the September 11, 2001, terrorist attacks]. They reveal some very disturbing practices.

Perhaps most upsetting is the government's use of "preventive detention"—the practice of imprisoning immigrants against whom there is no evidence of terrorist activity, purportedly as a means of preventing future attacks. Detention without evidence is not the hallmark of a free society.

Visitors to the U.S. were locked up for months in cells that were lit up 24 hours a day—merely because their visas had expired. They had no connection at all to terrorism, nor had they committed any crime. They were not informed of the charges against them for significant periods of time.

For weeks, some detainees had no access to a telephone—even to call a lawyer or family member. When concerned family members called, authorities refused to confirm whether a given individual even had been detained. . . .

Criticism from Within the Government

The OIG is an independent entity that reports to the Attorney General and to Congress. It has jurisdiction over the entire Department of Justice (DOJ)—including the FBI, the Federal Bureau of Prisons (BOP), and what was formerly known as the Immigration and Naturalization Service (INS), and is now part of the Office of Homeland Security.

The OIG issued a report in June 2003 providing a detailed analysis of the detention process used to hold 762 aliens accused of immigration violations as part of the DOJ's anti-terrorism initiatives.

The OIG's first report strongly criticizes DOJ, and the FBI in particular, for going beyond what even the attacks of September 11 required. For instance, OIG's first report states, "while the chaotic situation and the uncertainties surrounding the detainees' roles in the September 11 attacks and the potential for additional terrorism explain some of these problems they do not explain nor justify all of them. We believe that the Department and the FBI should consider these issues carefully in an effort to avoid similar problems in the future."

This criticism is all the more striking in that it comes from within the government itself.

After September 11, Attorney General John Ashcroft instructed the FBI and other federal law enforcement employees to use "every available law enforcement tool" to arrest persons who "participate in or lend support to, terrorist activities."

Harsh Confinement for Minor Immigration Violations

One such "tool" was the detention, in the 11 months after the attacks, of 762 aliens. The OIG's first report focuses on them.

The pretexts for these detentions were various immigration offenses, including overstaying their visas and entering the country illegally. The FBI feared some might be connected to the September 11 attacks, or to terrorism in general. But some were detained simply because the FBI was unable, at least initially, to determine whether they were connected to terrorism.

Among these were some who were targeted due to very vague leads (a landlord might find his Middle Eastern tenant "suspicious"). Others simply had the misfortune to be the roommate or coworker or someone who was under suspicion—in classic instances of unfair "guilt by association."

In one instance, law enforcement officers stopped three Middle Eastern men who were found to have plans for a public school in their car. But their employer verified that they were working on construction for a school, so that was entirely appropriate for them to have the plans. Nevertheless, the three men were detained.

Justifiably, then, the OIG faults the FBI for being overly broad in its decisions as to whom to detain. Its first report also revealed that the processes and criteria for deciding whether someone was a terrorist risk were ill defined and often arbitrary:

The first report thus criticized the "indiscriminate and haphazard manner in which the label of 'high interest,' 'of interest' or 'of undetermined interest' was applied to many aliens who had no connections to terrorism." And it stressed that, "the FBI should have taken more care to distinguish between aliens who it actually suspected . . . as opposed to aliens, while possibly guilty of violation [of] federal immigration law, had no connection to terrorism."

Unfortunately, once the labels were applied, however arbitrarily, they stuck—even to someone against whom there was no evidence at all. The process for allowing a detainee to clear himself, and thus free himself, was often slow and cumbersome.

Confinement Continued After Clearance

Only 2.6 percent were cleared within 3 weeks. The average length of time from arrest to clearance was 80 days. More than a quarter of the detainees were cleared only after 3 months. Some detainees remained in high security confinement even after the FBI had cleared them.

Granted, the government had cause to believe that the 762 detainees had violated federal immigration law. But prior to September 11, many such violations—such as the visa overstays—were common, and thus frequently overlooked.

Indeed, the OIG remarked that, "it is unlikely that most if not all of the individuals arrested would have been pursued by law enforcement authorities for these immigration violations but for the [September 11] investigation. Some appear to have been arrested more by virtue of chance encounters or tenuous connections to a [September 11] lead rather than any genuine indications of a possible connection with or possession of information about terrorist activity."

Moreover, under normal circumstances, the government's discovery of a possible immigration violation would not result in automatic detention. Instead, the alleged violator would learn the charge against him within 48 hours, and typically receive a formal Notice to Appear within 72 hours.

In contrast, the post–September 11 detainees, on average, did not receive their Notices for a week. Only 60 of them were timely served. Some did not receive notice of the charges against them for several weeks, or even a month.

Under normal circumstances, the alleged violator would receive a reasonably prompt immigration hearing. There, he would have a chance to mount a defense—a defense that the

Immigrants' Civil Liberties Must Be Protected

Under new Department of Justice policies, immigrants today can be arrested and held in secret for a lengthy period without charge, denied release on bond without effective recourse, and have their appeals dismissed following cursory or no review. They can be subjected to special, discriminatory registration procedures involving fingerprinting and lengthy questioning concerning their religious and political views. An immigrant spouse who is abused by her husband must fear deportation if she calls the local police. Asylum-seekers fleeing repressive regimes like those of the Taliban [in Afghanistan] or Saddam Hussein [in Iraq] may face mandatory detention, without any consideration of their individual circumstances.

There is a better approach. Instead of automatically viewing non-citizens with inherent suspicion, America should focus its resources on investigating and apprehending those who intend to commit acts of terrorism. America puts itself at greater risk by alienating immigrant communities, making immigrants distrustful and fearful of government.

The government must stop equating immigration with terrorism. Stepping up border screenings in a smart way can be part of a policy to make the United States safer. . . . Still, improving the "gatekeeper" function of immigration agencies is only one part, and not the most important one, of a balanced approach to national security that improves national security while respecting civil liberties.

Terrorism can only be stopped by improving the vulnerabilities in our intelligence system identified by the Joint Inquiry of the House and Senate intelligence committees into the September 11 [2001, terrorist] attacks. Immigration agents can stop terrorists if they have been told for whom to look by intelligence and law enforcement agencies; they should not be told to guess who is a danger on the basis of crude ethnic stereotypes.

Immigrants and new citizens make our country stronger, not weaker. They serve in our armed forces, as high-technology workers helping design the latest security technology, and as translators of critical intelligence information. They provide a bridge to world understanding, helping counter anti-American sentiment. If we isolate immigrants, we isolate ourselves—and make our country more vulnerable to terrorism.

Put simply, target terrorists, not immigrants.

Laura W. Murphy and Timothy H. Edgar, American Civil Liberties Union testimony before the House Judiciary Subcommittee on Immigration, Border Security, and Claims, May 8, 2003.

prompt Notice had allowed him to begin to prepare—with the aid of an attorney if he so chose.

All Detainees Were Under a "No Bond" Policy

Then, under normal circumstances, pending the hearing's outcome, the alleged violator would often be released on bond. But all 762 post–September 11 detainees came under a "Hold Until Cleared" policy, and a "no bond" policy.

Under this policy, the INS used boilerplate affidavits stating that national security concerns were involved to justify their opposition to bonds. When evidence was not available, they were told to ask for a continuance of the bond hearing, so they could at least interpose some delay.

Perhaps the most shocking segment of the OIG's first report relates to detainees who were classified as "high interest" by the FBI. This category may sound ominous—as if these detainees were all terrorists. But that wasn't at all the case.

In its report, the OIG "question[ed] the criteria (or lack thereof) the FBI used to make its initial designation of the potential danger posed by September 11 detainees." And it demonstrated how arbitrary the "high interest" designation often was: The arresting FBI agent could make this assessment without any guidance and based on the initial detainee information available at the time of the arrest.

Despite the hasty nature of the classification, it had huge consequences. For instance, 184 "high interest" detainees were confined in high security federal prisons as opposed to less restrictive INS detention facilities.

Moreover, 84 were held at the Metropolitan Detention Center (MDC) in Brooklyn, under highly restrictive conditions, including 23-hour-a-day lockdown. For many months, the lights in their cells were left on for 24 hours per day. When leaving their cells, they were handcuffed and placed in leg irons.

Some said they were verbally and physically abused. And indeed, despite denials from the BOP staff, the OIG found "significant evidence that the abuse occurred," and concluded "that the evidence indicates a pattern of abuse by some correctional officers against some September 11 detainees."

These detainees' status and location were withheld even

from attorneys and family members. They were allowed only one social telephone call per month. The vast majority had no legal counsel upon arriving at the prison and needed to secure counsel, but they were allowed only one legal telephone call per week—if that. (Evidence shows that the detainees may well not have had effective access to even that one call.)

For the first 3 weeks, during which a blackout was declared, no visitors (including attorney) were allowed at the MDC. Attorneys were also falsely told that their clients were not housed at the MDC, when they actually were.

Several detainees noted that the lists of pro bono attorneys provided to the detainees were handed out days or months after their arrivals. The lists also contained inaccuracies such as wrong telephone numbers.

In addition, detainees were often given no information about an administrative complaint process for reporting allegations of abuse, and no access to BOP handbooks for several months after their arrival. Some were merely given a 2-page summary of rules and procedures that did not mention the complaint process at all. . . .

On July 17, 2003, the OIG issued a second, follow-up report.

The USA Patriot Act had directed the OIG to "undertake a series of actions relating to claims of civil rights or civil liberties violations allegedly committed by DOJ employees." To do so, the OIG had established a Special Operations Branch in its Investigative Division, which received complaints of violation.

As of June 15, 2003, just before the second report was issued, the OIG had received a staggering 1073 complaints. However, only 272 fell within its jurisdiction (as opposed to that of other agencies, such as the Federal Aviation Administration, for example). And some complaints that were within OIG jurisdiction, were not within its USA Patriot Act mandate. Of the remaining complaints that were within both the OIG's jurisdiction and its mandate, 34 were deemed "credible" by the OIG.

Complaints of Abusive Behavior

Some newspaper accounts have suggested that the finding of only 34 credible complaints means there was not much of a problem. But it's important to remember that these complaints represented a significant percentage—more than 10%, and perhaps much higher than that—of those within the OIG's jurisdiction and mandate.

Moreover, these 34 complaints involved more than 34 individuals—some involve groups of detainees. For instance, twenty detainees alleged that a BOP correctional officer engaged in abusive behavior towards inmates.

Reportedly, the officer had ordered one Muslim inmate to remove his shirt so that the officer could use it to shine his shoes. A BOP internal investigatory report concluded that the allegations were unsubstantiated. But after OIG's investigation, the correctional officer admitted that he had initially been "less than completely candid" about the incident.

Here is a sampling of other complaints that are being investigated: An Egyptian citizen alleges that in a BOP facility, he was forced to undergo multiple and duplicative invasive body searches, denied the right to practice his religion, and forced to consume food prohibited by his religion. Another detainee alleges that an enforcement officer transferring him out of an INS facility, to another facility, held a loaded gun to his head and threatened him.

In another complaint—substantiated by the BOP—an inmate alleged that during a physical examination, a BOP physician told the inmate, "If I was in charge, I would execute every one of you . . . because of the crimes you all did." The same physician allegedly treated other inmates in a cruel and unprofessional manner.

Twenty of the 34 complaints were referred to the BOP directly. Of these, 16 are monitored referrals; the BOP must refer back to OIG.

These 20 complaints include allegations that BOP officials threatened to have an inmate's conditions of confinement changed unless the inmate cooperated with the government; abused inmates verbally by making slanderous remarks about Islam; placed an inmate in solitary confinement with a camera and a light that was constantly illuminated, and denied him legal assistance; made excessive searches of Muslim inmates' cells; and denied Muslim inmates access to television, radio, books and newspapers.

The second report applauds extensive efforts undertaken by the federal government to alert immigrants to their rights, and their ability to report civil rights violations. But it also suggests that many such violations occurred in the first place. Such civil rights violations that should not be tolerated in our justice system.

"More importantly, nowhere does the [Office of the Inspector General's] report claim that the Department of Justice violated the law—or that the detainees did not."

Detaining Immigrants to Prevent Future Terrorist Attacks Does Not Violate Their Civil Liberties

Bradford A. Berenson and Richard Klingler

Following the September 11, 2001, terrorist attacks, over seven hundred aliens were detained because U.S. authorities believed they had possible ties to terrorism. Bradford A. Berenson and Richard Klingler argue in the following viewpoint that the immigrant detention process reflected the government's best efforts to keep the country secure and protect civil liberties. Moreover, they insist that no laws were violated and that there were few documented instances of abuse. Bradford A. Berenson is a former associate White House counsel to President George W. Bush. Richard Klingler is an attorney in Washington, D.C.

As you read, consider the following questions:
1. In the authors' opinion, what were the most pointed concerns voiced in the Office of the Inspector General's report about the treatment of the detained immigrants?
2. What do the authors argue is the main reason to guard against exaggerated claims of abuse and unbalanced fear-mongering concerning the detainees?

Bradford A. Berenson and Richard Klingler, "Justice Served—Nabbing Illegal Aliens Isn't a Violation of Civil Rights," *Wall Street Journal*, June 9, 2003. Copyright © 2003 by Dow Jones & Company, Inc. All rights reserved. Reproduced by permission of the publisher and the authors.

Justice Department Inspector General Glenn Fine released a 198-page report . . . criticizing the department's handling of the post–Sept. 11 [2001] terrorism detainees. Media and interest-group reaction was swift and gleeful, treating the report as confirmation that the administration has trampled civil rights in the war on terrorism. Various articles featured claims by Anthony Romero, executive director of the ACLU [American Civil Liberties Union] that the report showed that "the war on terror quickly became a war on immigrants."

In fact, Mr. Fine's report did nothing of the sort. It examined the treatment of 762 indisputably illegal aliens, most of whom were later deported. His most pointed concerns arose from the treatment of 84 detainees at the Metropolitan Detention Center in Brooklyn, all of whom the FBI had classified as among the most high-risk terrorism-related detainees.

To be sure, the report documents a number of problems and areas in which the federal government's actions could have been made more fair or efficient. But the full report shows consistent efforts to meet the demands of security and civil liberties in the most trying circumstances.

Much of the discussion is actually quite mundane. The report describes bureaucratic problems and inefficiencies in carrying out a variety of complex tasks relating to the detainees, rather than wholesale or intentional violations of legal rights. More importantly, nowhere does the report claim that the Department of Justice violated the law—or that the detainees did not. It does not dispute that the department's detention policies were lawful or that all of the detainees were illegal aliens who had no right to be here at all.

If the problems identified in the inspector general's report are the worst things that we as a nation did in the immediate aftermath of the slaughter of thousands of American civilians in an epochal terrorist attack, we have done very well indeed.

Three Major Criticisms

The first of the three most salient criticisms leveled by the report relate to the Justice Department's policy of holding without bond all individuals detained as part of the post–Sept. 11 investigation until the FBI cleared them of connections to terrorism. Here, of course, Mr. Fine is forced to acknowledge that he "do[es] not criticize the decision to require FBI clearance of aliens to ensure that they had no connection to the September 11 attacks or terrorism in general." Instead, the gist of the report's complaint on this score is "that the FBI's clearance process was understaffed and not accorded sufficient priority."

Aggressive Detention Is Vital to Fighting Terrorism

As a nation of immigrants, America welcomes friends from other countries who wish to visit, to study, to work, become a part of our nation. But as September the 11th [2001, terrorist attacks] vividly illustrates, aliens also come to our country with the intent to do great evil. Just as we welcome America's friends, we will not allow our welcome to be abused by those who are America's enemies.

The Department of Justice will prevent aliens who engage in or support terrorist activity from entering our country. We will detain, prosecute, deport terrorist aliens who are already inside the nation's borders. America will not allow terrorists to use our hospitality as a weapon against us. . . .

Forty years ago, the Department of Justice, under Attorney General Robert Kennedy, undertook an extraordinary law enforcement campaign to root out and to dismantle organized crime. The Kennedy Justice Department, it is said, would arrest a mobster for spitting on the sidewalk, if it would aid in the war against organized crime.

In the war on terror, it is policy of this Justice Department to be equally aggressive. We will arrest and detain any suspected terrorist who has violated the law. If suspects are found not to have links to terrorism or not to have violated the law, they'll be released. But terrorists who are in violation of the law will be convicted, in some cases be deported, and in all cases be prevented from doing further harm to Americans.

Aggressive detention of lawbreakers and material witnesses is vital to preventing, disrupting, or delaying new attacks.

It is difficult for a person in jail or under detention to murder innocent people or to aid or abet in terrorism.

John Ashcroft, "Attorney General Ashcroft Outlines Foreign Terrorist Trading Task Force," U.S. Department of Justice, October 31, 2001.

But which special agents exactly would the inspector general have taken off of the active investigation of the Sept. 11

attacks to put on the task of trying to clear the names of those terrorism suspects that had already been removed from the streets? And which of the FBI's priorities in the immediate aftermath does Mr. Fine believe was too high?

The report itself notes that "within a week of the attacks, the FBI had assigned more than 7,000 employees to the task of tracking down anyone who had aided the terrorists and attempting to prevent additional attacks." Critical field offices were also preoccupied with investigating the [2001] anthrax attacks, the murder of *Wall Street Journal* reporter Daniel Pearl in Pakistan, searching for evidence in the debris of the World Trade Center and helping with security at the Winter Olympics. Keeping agents working on these matters rather than detainee clearance hardly seems unreasonable, even if that meant it took an average of 80 days to clear detainees rather than the "few weeks" some officials had initially expected.

In another section, the inspector general focuses on the department's delays in meeting its own objectives for notifying detainees of charges against them and deporting them. The stated notification goal of 72 hours, however, was not any sort of legal requirement. And yet, despite disruptions and difficult conditions, the INS [Immigration and Naturalization Service] still met its goal in 59% of cases and provided notice in most of the remainder shortly thereafter. As for delays in removal, the report's main criticism is that officials did not seek legal clarification soon enough—although when they did, the ruling supported their decision.

Abuse Was Not Considered Serious

The inspector general's third main criticism, while serious, is not as sensational as it sounds. The report found "physical and verbal abuse" directed at the 84 detainees at the MDC [Metropolitan Detention Center] in Brooklyn, but not at the hundreds of others at Passaic. While any abuse is wrong, the facts as outlined in the report do not support the more overheated criticisms. Officers subjected the MDC detainees, all of whom had been classified as high-risk by the FBI, to high security lock-downs, including limited time outside their cells. Officers moved detainees in shackles, and the most serious allegations concerned handcuffs that were too tight and officers who shoved detainees against walls upon intake or movement of prisoners.

Some officers also threatened detainees and called them names, including racial epithets. But the U.S. Attorney's Office investigated the allegations and found that evidence did not support criminal charges. In other words, particular corrections officers acted inappropriately in certain cases against a small group of detainees in one facility, but no serious injuries were substantiated and no broad government policy was implicated.

In context, it is remarkable that the allegations were not more extreme. In the immediate aftermath of Sept. 11, hardened corrections officers were overseeing illegal aliens suspected of being terrorists, in a facility within a subway's ride of the remnants of the World Trade Center.

Government Actions Were Legal and Limited

Comparing the report to how critics have characterized the detentions confirms that a vocal minority suffers from a loss of perspective. Critics and their media amplifiers have raised dramatic alarms about military tribunals, confinement of material witnesses, and other alleged misdeeds. In each case, the government's actions have proved to have a sound basis in law and a limited scope. Now, with this widely touted report, another cause celebre has evaporated.

Of course we all want the administration of justice to be as close to perfect as possible, and self-evaluation and self-criticism are valuable. But exaggerated claims and unbalanced fear-mongering have consequences. Crying wolf deprives critics of moral authority that would be valuable when a true injustice arises. Bureaucracies tend to inertia and are naturally cowed by public criticism, well-founded or not. They err on the side of delicacy rather than robustness. Given the threats at hand, robustness has its virtues.

Periodical Bibliography

The following articles have been selected to supplement the diverse views presented in this chapter.

Scott Berinato   "The Truth About Cyberterrorism," *CIO Magazine*, March 15, 2002.

Robert Bork   "Robert Bork on Civil Liberties After 9/11," *Free Republic*, July 4, 2003. www. freerepublic.com.

Richard A. Boswell   "Calamity of the Patriot," *Network News*, Spring 2002. www.nnirr.org.

Justin Durivage   "Racial Profiling Does Not Prevent Terrorism," *Student Life*, November 16, 2001. www.tsl.pomona.edu.

Wendy Kaminer   "Ashcroft's Lies," *American Prospect*, July 15, 2002.

Robert A. Levy   "Ethnic Profiling: A Rational and Moral Framework," *Cato Daily Commentary*, October 2, 2001. www.cato.org.

Joanne Mariner   "Indefinite Detention on Guantanamo," *FindLaw's Writ Legal Commentary*, May 28, 2002. www.writ.news.findlaw.com.

J.F.O. McAllister   "You Can't Kill Them All: Pre-emptive Strikes Against Terror Will Win Some Battles But Lose the War," *Time International*, August 4, 2003.

Charles V. Peña   "War on Terrorism or a War Against Americans?" *Capitol Hill Blue*, November 26, 2002. www.capitolhillblue.com.

Mark Pitcavage   "Afraid of Bugs: Assessing Our Attitudes Towards Biological and Chemical Terrorism," *Militia Watchdog*, February 12, 1999. www.militia-watchdog.org.

Jason L. Riley   "Racial Profiling and Terrorism," *Wall Street Journal*, October 24, 2001. www.opinionjournal.com.

Debbie Schlussel   "Why We Need Racial Profiling," *WorldNet Daily*, May 18, 2001. www.worldnetdaily.com.

Susan Sontag   "How Grief Turned into Humbug: Real War Has a Beginning and an End," *New Statesman*, September 16, 2002.

University of Michigan Documents Center	"America's War on Terrorism," October 2, 2003. www.lib.umich.edu/govdocs/usterror. html.
Gore Vidal	"The New War on Freedom," *San Francisco Chronicle*, April 19, 2002. www.independent.org.
William J. Watkins Jr.	"Combating Terrorism and the Lessons of 1798," December 6, 2001. The Independent Institute, www.independent.org.

CHAPTER 3

Will the Domestic Antiterrorism Measures Make Americans Safer?

Chapter Preface

Mandatory for many years in European countries such as England, France, and Germany, national identification cards have been overwhelmingly rejected by the American people and the U.S. Congress. However, the terrorist attacks of September 11, 2001, have inspired renewed interest in the creation of national ID cards. Many argue that the ability to positively identify all Americans will make everyone safer. The key to a national ID system, according to Larry Ellison, chairman and CEO of Oracle Software, is a massive database of information. He points out that the government currently maintains many such databases because it issues Social Security cards, driver's licenses, pilot's licenses, passports, visas, and other necessary documents. According to Ellison, using existing Social Security or state driver's license databases would be a good starting point for the creation of a national ID system.

Ellison has offered Oracle Software free of charge to the government to help consolidate these databases and make national ID cards a viable weapon in the war against terrorism. Attorney General John Ashcroft is considering the offer. Ellison claims, "The single thing we could do to make life tougher for terrorists would be to ensure that all the information in the myriad government databases was integrated into a single national file." Attorney and author Alan M. Dershowitz agrees with Ellison and advocates a voluntary identity card with a microchip that could be matched to the holder's fingerprint. He maintains, "It could be an effective tool for preventing terrorism, reducing the need for other law-enforcement mechanisms—especially racial and ethnic profiling—that pose even greater dangers to civil liberties."

However, Katie Corrigan, legislative counsel on privacy for the American Civil Liberties Union, contends that a "national ID card will encourage increased racial profiling as well as other egregious violations of civil liberties without making Americans safer or terrorism less likely to occur." A national ID card would not be an effective counterterrorism measure, she argues. Instead, such a system could "divert resources from other counterterrorism activities and create a government bureaucracy that would undermine basic rights." Further, critics such as Corrigan contend that massive information databases would threaten the privacy of average Americans and impinge on Americans' freedom to move around freely in their communities. Corrigan argues that a national ID system would violate one freedom that most clearly defines America: the right to be left alone, especially by the government.

The debate engendered by national ID card proposals is just one of many surrounding America's war on terrorism. Authors in the following chapter examine other measures being proposed and implemented in an effort to make America safer.

"The primary mission of the Office of Homeland Security has been to . . . secure the United States from terrorist attacks and threats."

The Department of Homeland Security Will Make Americans Safer

Tom Ridge

The following viewpoint was originally given as remarks to the National Association of Broadcasters National Education Foundation on June 10, 2002, in support of the creation of a new Homeland Security Department. In it, Tom Ridge argues that because the Department of Homeland Security would bring together the responsibilities of over one hundred different governmental agencies, it would provide the national security structure necessary to protect Americans. Ridge insists that without the new department, scattered responsibilities and poor communication will make it impossible to protect the United States. Tom Ridge is the director of the Department of Homeland Security. The new department was created in November 2002.

As you read, consider the following questions:

1. Name three responsibilities that will be assigned to the Department of Homeland Security, according to Ridge.
2. Which federal agency is in charge of the national pharmaceutical stockpile, according to the author?
3. Why did President Harry Truman reorganize the military after World War II, in the author's opinion?

Tom Ridge, address to the National Association of Broadcasters National Education Foundation, 2002 Service to America Summit, June 10, 2002.

The nine months since the terrorist attacks [on September 11, 2001] have been a great time to be an American, in spite of the horror and the tragedy associated with the attacks. We have learned so much about what this country and its people are all about.

It is one of the most important, if not the most important, stories of our lifetimes. It's the story of how we protect American lives and the American way of life, the most important job of government.

Last week [June 2002], President [George W.] Bush announced a major change in how we will do that job. The President has proposed a new Department of Homeland Security.[1]

The new department will be commissioned and tasked to protect our borders and airports and seaports and to monitor visitors to this country; to overseas preparedness and to help train and equip first-responders; to address the threat from weapons of mass destruction, and turn policies into action through regional drills; to map our Nation's critical infrastructure so we can learn where the great vulnerabilities lie and take action to reduce them; to synthesize and analyze homeland security intelligence from multiple sources, so we can separate fact from fiction and identify trends that help us deter and catch terrorists; and finally, to communicate threats and actions to those who need to know—governors, mayors, law enforcement officials, business owners, and the public.

Scattered Responsibility

Today, no single agency calls homeland security its sole or even its primary mission. Instead, responsibility is scattered among more than 100 separate government organizations. Consequently, despite the best efforts of the best public servants, our response is often ad hoc. We don't always have the kind of alignment of authority and responsibility with accountability that gets things done. This creates situations that would be comical if the threat were not so serious.

Are you the captain of a foreign flagship that entered U.S. waters? You could meet agents from Customs, the Immigration and Naturalization Service (INS), Coast Guard, or the

1. The Department of Homeland Security was created in November 2002.

Agriculture Department, each of whom might have jurisdiction over some portion of your ship. And even though the Coast Guard has the authority to act as an agent for the other three, they often defer to their Federal colleagues.

The same thing happens if you're taking a car or truck across a border—you can see the INS or Customs, or perhaps the Border Patrol or Agriculture or somebody else there. One opens the hood, one looks for people, one checks the baggage, one opens the trunk. Again, we need to do a better job of targeting those resources, perhaps in crosstraining, to deploy these men and women and the technology that they have at their disposal in a much more effective way.

Let me give you another example. Say you live near a nuclear power facility, and you want to obtain potassium iodine in an emergency—and some States are actually in the process of distributing some. If you live within a 10-mile radius of the plant, the Nuclear Regulatory Commission regulates the distribution of this very important drug. If you live outside the circle, the Federal Emergency Management Agency [FEMA] regulates the distribution. But of course, if you live within 10 miles of a nuclear weapons facility, it's the Department of Energy that distributes the drug. And oh, by the way, to add one more layer, if there isn't enough potassium iodine to go around, then the Department of Health and Human Services is in charge of the national pharmaceutical stockpile.

Eliminating Confusion

These men and women go to work every day. They're patriots all, and they work very hard to comply with the law and do what they're told to do, according to the law and the regulations and the direction of their agency. But clearly a situation like that shouldn't be so cumbersome, shouldn't be so complex. It is confusing, to say the least. We need to eliminate as much of the confusion as possible.

The Department of Homeland Security will have a single mission. As the President reminds all of us, it is his most important job, and the most important job of the Federal Government: Protect the American people and our way of life from terrorism. And it will have a single, clear line of authority to get the job done. It will bring together everyone under the same roof, working toward the same goal and pushing in the same direction.

Let me give you another example. Right now, many governmental organizations collect intelligence for a variety of purposes. The most prominent are the CIA and the FBI, but obviously you have several in the Department of Defense, the National Security Agency. You've got the Drug Enforcement [Administration]. INS collects intelligence, Customs collects intelligence, Coast Guard collects intelligence. You have multiple agencies out there that gather information and intelligence.

No single agency conducts a comprehensive analysis of that entire universe of data. No single agency is charged with that task.

That would change. Not only will the department have access to the data, but that department will be able to fuse it, analyze it for threats, and then map those threats against vulnerabilities, which the department will also be responsible to assess. We can then put out the threat advisories or call for increased security measures to meet the threat. Basically, the department will be able to put together all of the pieces of the puzzle and, depending on what the picture shows, take the requisite action.

A National Strategy

Since day one, the primary mission of the Office of Homeland Security has been to develop a comprehensive national strategy to secure the United States from terrorist attacks and threats. This proposal is the centerpiece of that national strategy. It gives us the structure that we need in order to implement the national strategy.

I know conflict usually makes for far better news than consensus. And any reform this far-reaching will certainly have its share of both conflict and criticism. The conflicts are particularly sensitive in a town as turf-conscious as Washington, D.C. But as I said on day one, the only turf we should be worried about protecting is the turf we stand on. And by and large, the people who serve this President have taken that message to heart.

And I'm confident, by the way, based on numerous conversations I've had with Republicans and Democrats on the Hill, that they share this President's commitment to getting this done sooner rather than later. If we can work together, presidential leadership with legislative leadership, and get it done by the end of the year, as the President has suggested and hoped, I think it would be an extraordinary accomplishment.

The Department of Homeland Security Provides Flexibility

The [terrorist] attacks on September 11th [2001] changed the everyday lives of Americans. As a result of these attacks, our country is now at war with an invisible enemy that lurks in the shadows. We face the real possibility of additional attacks of a similar or even greater magnitude. Terrorists around the world are conspiring to obtain chemical, biological, and nuclear weapons with the express intent of killing large numbers of Americans. We saw on September 11th that terrorists will use unconventional means to deliver their terror.

These new times require new thinking. Creating a Department of Homeland Security will give the government the flexibility necessary to make the right decisions that are needed to protect the American people.

Todd Tiahrt, U.S. House of Representatives debate on the Homeland Security Act of 2002, July 26, 2002.

[FEMA Director] Joe Allbaugh said at a Cabinet meeting where the President announced his plans, "Mr. President, you came to Washington as a change agent and we're change agents, too—otherwise, why are we here?" It's a huge change, a sea change, nothing like it since Harry Truman. And I believe the Executive and Legislative Branches together will get it done.

Now, we all know that change can be fairly uncomfortable. It's been said that it is always easier to create new government than it is to reorganize old government. The President's reform touches nearly every Cabinet department, and will affect nearly 170,000 Federal employees. But we need to seek a better fit between the job at hand and the agencies with the matching core competencies in the field. And I want to assure them that they will have the satisfaction of going to work every day knowing they're protecting the American people and our way of life.

No New Bureaucracy

I also want to reassure taxpayers that we are not creating a new Federal bureaucracy. We're not creating a new government agency in the sense that there are 170,000 new employees that will be going to work for the Federal Government. The President said we need to make the existing government work better and to focus on efficiency and effectiveness if we're to consolidate and streamline our homeland security responsibilities.

The President and I believe the American people need a single department that can partner with States and localities. In the President's directive creating the position of Advisor to the President for Homeland Security, one of the tasks given to our office was to design and implement a national strategy—not just a Federal strategy. A national strategy, by implication, means we have to work and do a better job not just within our Federal agencies, but we have to tie ourselves together with State and local government and the private sector as well.

We need to make this department a clearinghouse for many of the best practices that we believe can be deployed to prevent terrorism. And certainly we need to do a better job of preparing our country, building up capacity to respond to an attack, if it occurs.

We can never eliminate the threat completely. We can never eliminate the notion of surprise, of terrorist attack, particularly in a society that's as open and as free and as diverse and as large as we are in the United States of America. But I believe we can significantly reduce the vulnerability to terrorism and terrorist attack over time. We can give Americans greater peace of mind, convenience, and commerce.

Homeland Security Touches Everyone

Homeland security is not an inside-the-Beltway story. It encompasses the air we breathe, the food we eat, the water we drink, the energy we use, critical infrastructure everywhere. It affects us every time we board a plane or visit the office or log onto our computers. It touches everyone's lives.

Half a century ago, President [Harry] Truman saw a need to reorganize the military, in spite of the victory in World

War II, to meet the new threat, the Soviet threat. Back then, the Army and Navy and other military organizations had separate, independent commands. Truman looked at the lessons learned from Pearl Harbor and from our prosecution of the war, and he said: "In the theaters of operation, we went further in the direction of unity by establishing unified commands. But we never had comparable unified direction or command in Washington." Sounds familiar.

He added: "It is now time to discard obsolete organizational forms, and to provide for the future the soundest, the most effective, and the most economical kind of structure for our armed forces." Truman pushed for the creation of a unified Department of Defense, a Central Intelligence Agency to learn about the threat, and a National Security Council to analyze the threat. He got all three.

When told it couldn't be done, he said simply, in typical Truman, straightforward, plain language, "It has to be done." His efforts turned the U.S. military into the most powerful force for freedom the world has ever seen. And though he didn't live to see it, his vision and his reorganization helped bring down the Berlin Wall and end the Cold War, a goal many, many people in the 1950s and the 1960s thought impossible.

It's time for us to take the lessons learned from 9/11 and from our war on terrorism and apply them to homeland security. We may not see victories in our lifetimes either, but if we build the foundation now, I'm confident America can do the impossible and make history once again.

*"Government reorganizations . . . can have
a deleterious effect not just on the
functioning of government but on our
safety and liberty as well."*

The Department of Homeland Security Will Not Make Americans Safer

Ron Paul

The following viewpoint was originally given as testimony before the U.S. House of Representatives on July 26, 2002, in opposition to the creation of the Department of Homeland Security. Ron Paul argues in it that reorganizing the federal government to create the new department is misguided and will not result in greater safety for Americans. Further, he maintains that creation of the new department will cost taxpayers $3 billion and allow the executive branch to spend money appropriated by Congress in unauthorized ways. Paul insists that the Department of Homeland Security will make many federal agencies less effective, less efficient, and more intrusive. Ron Paul is a member of the U.S. House of Representatives. The Department of Homeland Security was created in November 2002.

As you read, consider the following questions:
1. In Paul's opinion, which government agencies critical to defense of the United States are missing from the consolidation and reorganization?
2. What issues does Paul maintain must be dealt with before Americans can expect improved homeland security?

Ron Paul, testimony before the U.S. House of Representatives, Washington, DC, July 26, 2002.

As many commentators have pointed out, the creation of this new department [the Department of Homeland Security] represents the largest reorganization of Federal agencies since the creation of the Department of Defense in 1947.[1] Unfortunately, the process by which we are creating this new department bears little resemblance to the process by which the Defense Department was created.

Congress began hearings on the proposed department of defense in 1945—two years before President [Harry] Truman signed legislation creating the new department into law. Despite the lengthy deliberative process through which Congress created the new department, turf battles and logistical problems continued to bedevil the military establishment, requiring several corrective pieces of legislation. In fact, the Goldwater-Nichols Department of Defense Reorganization Act of 1986 was passed to deal with problems stemming from the 1947 law. The experience with the Department of Defense certainly suggests the importance of a more deliberative process in the creation of this new agency.

This current proposed legislation suggests that merging 22 government agencies and departments—comprising nearly 200,000 Federal employees—into one department will address our current vulnerabilities. I do not see how this can be the case.

If we are presently under terrorist threat, it seems to me that turning 22 agencies upside down, sparking scores of turf wars, and creating massive logistical and technological headaches—does anyone really believe that even simple things like computer and telephone networks will be up and running in the short term?—is hardly the way to maintain the readiness and focus necessary to defend the United States.

Americans Will Be Vulnerable

What about vulnerabilities while Americans wait for this massive new bureaucracy to begin functioning as a whole even to the levels at which its component parts were functioning before this legislation was taken up? Is this a risk we can afford to take? Also, isn't it a bit ironic that in the name

1. The Department of Homeland Security was created in November 2002.

of "homeland security" we seem to be consolidating everything except the government agencies most critical to the defense of the United States, the multitude of intelligence agencies that make up the intelligence community?

I come from a coastal district in Texas. The Coast Guard and its mission are important to us. The chairman of the committee of jurisdiction over the Coast Guard has expressed strong reservations about the plan to move the Coast Guard into the new department. Recently my district was hit by the flooding in Texas, and we relied upon the Federal Emergency Management Agency to again provide certain services. Additionally, as a district close to our border, much of the casework performed in my district offices relates to requests made to the Immigration and Naturalization Service [INS].

There has been a difference of opinion between committees of jurisdiction and the administration in regard to all these functions. In fact, the President's proposal was amended in no fewer than a half dozen of the dozen committees to which it was originally referred.

My coastal district also relies heavily on shipping. Our ports are essential for international trade and commerce. Last year [2001], over one million tons of goods was moved through just one of the ports in my district. However, questions remain about how the mission of the Customs Service will be changed by this new department.

The New Department Will Cost $3 Billion

For me to vote this bill would amount to giving my personal assurance that the creation of this new department will not adversely impact the fashion in which the Coast Guard and Customs Service provide the services which my constituents have come to rely upon. Based on the expedited process we have followed with this legislation, I do not believe I can give such assurance.

We have also received a Congressional Budget Office cost estimate suggesting that it will cost no less than $3 billion just to implement this new department. That is $3 billion that could be spent to capture those responsible for the attacks of September 11 [2001] or to provide tax relief to the families of the victims of that attack. It is $3 billion that could perhaps be better spent protecting against future attacks, or simply to meet the fiscal needs of our government.

The Department of Homeland Security Threatens Americans

The values and constitutional liberties of this Nation are not only threatened by terrorists but by the possibilities of a Federal Government without proper checks and balances. For black Americans, the latter threat is much more conceivable than the former. I want to see the Nation combat these despicable terrorists acts, but not by completely centralizing the power of the Federal Government, or trampling on our civil liberties, or not protecting Federal employees' rights.

My conscience will not permit me to agree with this bill's construction of the Department of Homeland Security. I will not agree with legislation to strip civil liberties. I will not agree with a contract that will deny workers their rights and proper recourse for wrong done towards them. I will not be silent to the ills of this bill, even in the midst of a daunting and scary future, which has bred fear through us all.

Carolyn C. Kilpatrick, U.S. House of Representatives debate on the Homeland Security Act of 2002, July 26, 2002.

Since those attacks this Congress has gone on a massive spending spree. Spending three billion additional dollars now, simply to rearrange offices and command structures, is not a wise move. In fact, Congress is actually jeopardizing the security of millions of Americans by raiding the Social Security trust fund to rearrange deck chairs and give big spenders yet another department on which to lavish pork-barrel spending.

The way the costs of this department have skyrocketed before the department is even open for business leads me to fear that this will become yet another justification for Congress to raid the Social Security trust fund in order to finance pork-barrel spending. This is especially true in light of the fact that so many questions remain regarding the ultimate effect of these structural changes.

Moreover, this legislation will give the Executive Branch the authority to spend money appropriated by Congress in ways Congress has not authorized. This clearly erodes constitutionally mandated congressional prerogatives relative to control of Federal spending.

The airlines are bailed out and given guaranteed insurance against all threats. We have made the airline industry a public utility that gets to keep its profits and pass on its losses to the taxpayers, like Amtrak and the post office. Instead of more ownership responsibility, we get more government controls. I am reluctant, to say the least, to give any new powers to bureaucrats who refuse to recognize the vital role free citizens exercising their Second Amendment rights play in homeland security.

No Improvement in Security

Government reorganizations, though generally seen as benign, can have a deleterious effect not just on the functioning of government but on our safety and liberty as well. The concentration and centralization of authority that may result from today's efforts should give us all reason for pause. But the current process does not allow for pause. Indeed, it militates toward rushing decisions without regard to consequence.

Furthermore, this particular reorganization, in an attempt to provide broad leeway for the new department, undermines our congressional oversight function. Abrogating our constitutionally mandated responsibilities so hastily now also means that future administrations will find it much easier to abuse the powers of this new department to violate constitutional liberties.

Perhaps a streamlined, reconfigured Federal Government with a more clearly defined and limited mission focused on protecting citizens and their freedoms could result from this reorganization, but right now it seems far more likely that the opposite will occur. That is why I must oppose creation of this new department.

Until we deal with the substance of the problem—serious issues of American foreign policy about which I have spoken out for years, and important concerns with our immigration policy in light of the current environment—attempts such as we undertake today at improved homeland security will amount to, more or less, rearranging deck chairs—or perhaps more accurately office chairs in various bureaucracies.

Until we are prepared to have serious and frank discussions of policy, this body will not improve the security of American citizens and their property. I stand ready to have that debate, but unfortunately this bill does nothing to begin the debate and nothing substantive to protect us. At best it will provide an illusion of security, and at worst these unanswered questions will be resolved by the realization that entities such as the Customs Service, Coast Guard, and INS will be less effective, less efficient, more intrusive, and mired in more bureaucratic red tape.

*"Political correctness keeps almost every . . .
leader in our nation from endorsing strict
control over our borders, . . . control that
would bar the admittance of anyone
deemed potentially dangerous to our
homeland security."*

Restricting Immigration Will Make Americans Safer

John D. Perazzo

In the following viewpoint John D. Perazzo argues that the influx of illegal immigrants into America due to improperly guarded borders and lax enforcement of existing immigration laws makes the United States vulnerable to terrorism and compromises the safety of all Americans. He claims that illegal aliens have participated in almost every major Islamic terrorist attack committed in the United States. Unless illegal immigration is stopped, he contends, there is no chance of stopping terrorism in the United States. John D. Perazzo is a columnist for FrontPageMagazine.com and the author of *The Myths That Divide Us: How Lies Have Poisoned American Race Relations.*

As you read, consider the following questions:
1. According to the author, what percentage of all cargo containers on U.S.-bound ships is inspected?
2. What two loopholes do illegal aliens most often use to "adjust their status," in Perazzo's opinion?
3. How often were simulated guns and explosives successfully smuggled past security checkpoints at thirty-two airports, according to the author?

The single greatest threat to the lives of America's 280 million people remains, to this day, utterly unaddressed by political leaders afraid to lose the votes of ethnicity lobbies that would be "offended" by tighter government controls of our nation's borders. It is that simple.

Consequently, illegal aliens are free to enter our country—virtually without encumbrance—by land, sea, and air. Michelle Malkin's startling new book *Invasion* documents how truly grave the danger of illegal immigration is, and how appallingly meek has been our government's response to the problem.

Malkin points out, for instance, that seven months ago the US Coast Guard received intelligence information that some twenty-five al Qaeda–linked Islamic extremists had entered our country as stowaways aboard commercial cargo vessels docking in Florida, Georgia, and California ports. Yet it is by no means surprising that some of the world's most bloodthirsty monsters were able to sneak into our midst in this manner. Barely 3 percent of all cargo containers on US-bound ships are inspected upon arrival. According to Michael O'Hanlon of the Brookings Institution, that fact "may be our single greatest vulnerability that we have not yet made much progress toward addressing."

We know that at least two of the terrorist conspirators who plotted the foiled Los Angeles International Airport millennium bombing illegally entered the US aboard ships from Algeria. The INS [Immigration and Naturalization Service] reports that at the Norfolk, Virginia seaport *alone*, the crews of at least forty foreign cargo vessels have been permitted ashore without proper authorization *since* [*the September 11, 2001, terrorist attacks*]. Such a state of affairs would hardly even qualify for a television script, as no intelligent audience could realistically be expected to believe it.

For aspiring terrorists prone to seasickness, there's plenty of elbow room to be found along the land routes. Our country's 4,000-mile border with Canada is guarded by fewer than 400 Border Patrol agents—barely one for every ten miles. Half a world away, the US military has been deployed to seal the border between Afghanistan and Pakistan in an effort to prevent the escape of al Qaeda terrorists, but political correctness prevents us from similarly protecting the borders on the very doorstep of our nation. And as we learned so painfully on 9/11, terrorists in our midst can harm us much more than can their counterparts in the Afghan mountains.

Minimal Inspection at the Border

But would-be terrorists don't need to go far out of their way to find unpatrolled locations where they can sneak into the US. They can casually saunter—with very little likelihood of detection—across the very same roads and bridges that everyone else uses. Indeed 99 percent of the 8.5 million motor vehicles and trains that crossed the Buffalo-Niagara border bridges [in 2001] were permitted to enter our country without inspection. In the south the situation is much the same, as Malkin explains: "[Osama bin Laden terrorist] operatives can pay cheap prices for escorts, join global smuggling rings, . . . or ride the rails undetected from Mexico along with hundreds of thousands of other 'undocumented workers.'"

Even in the comparatively few cases where illegal aliens are identified and ordered deported, the violators are generally released on own recognizance—rendering their deportation rulings toothless and hollow. The *Washington Post* reports that at least 314,000 illegal aliens who have been ordered deported—including 6,000 Middle Easterners—have simply disappeared and cannot be located.

Predictably, the self-destructive insanity of our immigration policy has not escaped the notice of aspiring illegal immigrants. As a result, they have become emboldened to the point of shamelessness, in some cases actually suing the US for failing to provide water stations along their illegal routes into our country. Presumably, those who break our immigration laws have a right not to get thirsty while doing so.

Incredible though it may seem, our immigration authorities have been cowed by such brazenness, as evidenced by INS commissioner James Ziglar's recent announcement of the activation of several thirty-foot-tall "rescue beacons" with strobe lights and alarm buttons that sick or weary illegals can use to call for help. Malkin reports that a similar initiative will station horses and hovercraft in remote regions of America's southern border, so as to protect illegal immigrants from drowning or getting lost. Could there be a more blatant slap in the face of American taxpayers, than to have them fund such disgraceful boondoggles? These are the symptoms of a nation gone mad.

The legal loopholes available to those seeking to enter our midst and plot our eventual doom are virtually limitless. Consider, for instance, the widespread prevalence of marriage fraud. A would-be terrorist can marry an American to obtain legal residence, and eventually even citizenship. Among those who have done precisely this was El Sayyid Nosair, who married an American-born Muslim woman just as he faced possible deportation for having overstayed his visa. Nosair not only went on to become a naturalized US citizen, but also to help carry out the 1993 World Trade Center (WTC) bombing.

Marriage Fraud Is Widespread

Similarly, bin Laden aide Ali Mohammed's route to citizenship began with his marriage to an American woman, after which he helped execute the 1998 US embassy bombings in Africa. Khalid Abu al Dahab became a citizen after marrying no fewer than three American women, and thereafter distinguished himself by joining the aforementioned Mohammed in plotting the embassy bombings. The *San Francisco Chronicle* describes Dahab as "a one-man communications hub" for al Qaeda, not only recruiting American citizens of Middle Eastern descent for bin Laden's network, but also sending cash and phony passports to terrorists around the world from his California apartment.

The pitiful saga does not end there. Malkin reminds us that eight Middle Eastern men who plotted to bomb various New York City landmarks also married American citizens in order to obtain permanent legal residence. Even Osama bin Laden's personal secretary married an American in 1985 and became a naturalized citizen four years later. It is enough to demoralize anyone who truly loves this land.

Of course, for the commitment-phobic terrorist who prefers not to marry, there is always the option of invoking political asylum—whose original intent was to offer safe haven to those fleeing political tyranny. Tragically, our country's generosity toward that end is habitually abused and exploited by those committed to destroying us—people like murderer Mir Aimal Kansi and WTC bomb plotters Ramzi Yousef and Sheik Omar Abdel Rahman. Each day, untold numbers of asylum seekers such as these are released on their own recognizance and promptly disappear. Their asylum hearings are often delayed for many months, by which point they are no longer traceable. According to a 2002 General Accounting Office report, a preliminary review examining 5,000 petitions for asylum found a 90-percent fraud rate. In a more comprehensive follow-up analysis of 1,500 of those petitions, only *one* could be verified as legitimate. These figures, as documented by Malkin, are nothing short of astonishing.

Trow. © 1997 by Copley News Service. Reproduced by permission.

Yet another escape hatch for illegal aliens is to simply wait for a general amnesty to "adjust their status." The 1993 WTC bomber Mahmud Abouhalima demonstrated how to do this quite effectively. Having come to the US with a six-month tourist visa in 1985, he overstayed his visa and patiently waited for Congress to grant amnesty for illegals the following year.

Moreover, a federal program allows those who violate our immigration laws to avoid potential legal hassles by simply paying a $1,000 fee to—again—"adjust their status" and gain permanent residence. More than half a million illegals took advantage of this loophole between 1994 and 1997. Incredibly, some of our nation's most eminent political figures—in both major parties—seem oblivious to the dangers of this policy. A mere ten months ago [February 2002] Richard Gephardt asserted that "we need to expand and extend" such programs. Senator Ted Kennedy echoed Gephardt's call for a "meaningful extension" of the program. President Bush joined the chorus as well, characterizing the law as a safeguard for "family values."

High Proportion of Terrorists Are Illegal Aliens

Such words are uttered notwithstanding the fact that illegal aliens have, as Steven Camarota of the Center for Immigration Studies explains, "taken part in almost every major attack on American soil perpetrated by Islamic terrorists, including the first attack on the World Trade Center, the Millenium plot, the plot to bomb the New York subway, and the attacks of 9/11." Further, those words are uttered despite the fact that illegal aliens of all nationalities comprise an astonishingly high proportion of convicted criminals in several American states. They are 24 percent of New York State's prisoners, for instance. In California the figure approaches 15 percent.

We are a nation that too readily turns a blind eye to the malevolence that surrounds us. Our refusal to take seriously the current terrorist threat is evident even in the airline industry—the very realm wherein bin Laden's henchmen attacked us on 9/11. For example, in a study conducted at 32 airports between November 2001 and February 2002, when airports were on their highest alert, undercover government testers successfully snuck knives past security checkpoints 70 percent of time; for simulated explosives, their success rate was 60 percent, and for guns 30 percent. A similar study conducted seven months ago [June 2002] by the Transportation Security Administration found that simulated guns and explosives were successfully smuggled past security checkpoints at 32 airports about once in every four attempts.

These staggering numbers are not themselves the problem. They are symptomatic of a mindset that is unwilling to fight evil with tireless, focused resolve. Thus we have effectively rendered ourselves helpless in the face of potential future attacks by terrorists *already in our midst*, who are merely awaiting an opportune moment to strike. A December 14 [2002] *New York Post* story reported that, in the event of a threatened city transit strike, NYPD officers would aggressively inspect vehicles deemed capable of hauling explosives designed to destroy the city's bridges and tunnels. Such catastrophes are quite obviously within the realm of possibility, yet political correctness keeps almost every political leader in our nation from endorsing strict control over our borders, a control that would bar the admittance of anyone deemed potentially dangerous to our homeland security.

One might have thought that a calamity like 9/11 would have opened our Congressional representatives' eyes to the need for greater safeguards. But alas, not enough people died to spur them into meaningful action. Perhaps when a future attack inflicts a death toll that exceeds 9/11 by a hundredfold or a thousandfold, we will finally hear them acknowledge what any thinking person understands already: If we do not end illegal immigration immediately, there's really no point in getting all worked up about Social Security, 401-K's, school vouchers, or any other issue whose relevance is founded upon an expectation that the sun will rise tomorrow.

"Of all the migration policy changes since the terrorist attacks, the diminished US refugee program threatens to cause the greatest suffering while yielding the fewest security benefits."

Restricting Immigration Will Not Make Americans Safer

Donald Kerwin

Restricting illegal immigration will not reduce terrorism because most terrorists enter the country with legal visas, Donald Kerwin, executive director of the Catholic Legal Immigration Network contends in the following viewpoint. He argues that restricting the immigration of refugees will cause the most suffering while providing the least additional security from terrorism. To be successful, any antiterrorism measures the government enacts must reflect the basic principles of the United States, which includes providing refuge for people fleeing political persecution. To do less, he maintains, would sacrifice America's core values without enhancing security for anyone.

As you read, consider the following questions:
1. What does the author argue is the most difficult and unlikely path for a terrorist trying to enter the United States?
2. What was the outcome of the Department of Justice's announcement that it would begin enforcing a law requiring immigrants to report a change of address within ten days of moving, in the author's opinion?

Donald Kerwin, "National Security and Immigrant Rights," *The Nation*, December 19, 2002. Copyright © 2002 by The Nation Magazine/The Nation Company, Inc. Reproduced by permission.

The debate over how to protect the United States from terrorism while safeguarding its guiding values rages with particular intensity in immigrant communities. The federal government has directed more than thirty antiterror measures at select groups of immigrants since [the terrorist attacks of] September 11, 2001. Not all these measures endanger core rights. Nonetheless, one questions how some of them meaningfully protect the public.

Of all the migration policy changes since the terrorist attacks, the diminished US refugee program threatens to cause the greatest suffering while yielding the fewest security benefits. The US Committee for Refugees counted 14.9 million refugees—the most desperate of migrants—worldwide in 2001. In October 2001, the United States suspended refugee admissions pending a security review of its program. Despite a presidential designation to admit 70,000 refugees in fiscal year 2002, only 27,000 were allowed to enter, and refugee admissions in the first months of fiscal year 2003 continue at a trickle. The refugee process is perhaps the most difficult and unlikely path a terrorist could take to reach the United States. The September 11 terrorists opted for a far easier route, i.e., they entered legally on temporary visas. Despite this reality, the Administration has failed to explain why decreasing refugee admissions will make us safer.

Other putative antiterror measures seem more reasonable at first glance. In July 2002, the Department of Justice (DOJ) announced plans to enforce a law that requires immigrants to report changes of address within ten days after they move. Law enforcement officials could definitely benefit from a database with the correct addresses of the 31 million foreign-born persons in the United States, or of every US citizen for that matter. However, the change-of-address plan will not accomplish this goal. Among other problems, it ignores the INS [Immigration and Naturalization Service] track record of losing and misplacing documents. INS reports collecting more than 2 million lost documents, 200,000 of them change-of-address cards. In addition, according to the General Accounting Office (GAO) the INS "lacks adequate procedures and controls to ensure that the alien address information it receives is completely processed." Since DOJ's announcement,

Critics say the [new national security] measures could subject
law-abiding immigrants to discrimination or allow for false
accusations. . . . For example, the attorney general would be
able to certify someone as deportable for terrorist ties if officials have "reason to believe" the individual is a threat to
national security.

Civil libertarians note that wartime fears have led to extreme
crackdowns on immigrants in the past. . . . "It is a recurring
theme in United States history that when threats have been
perceived, there has been a pattern of harsher enforcement
against people who are not American citizens, or who are perceived as not being fully 'American,'" said Hiroshi Motomura,
a professor at the University of Colorado School of Law.

Jonathan Peterson and Patrick J. McDonnell, *Los Angeles Times*, September 23, 2001.

the agency has received an estimated 700,000 change-of-
address notices. Not surprising, it has not processed the vast
majority of these forms. GAO also pointed out that immigrants who do not wish to be detected "would not likely comply" with this requirement. This would certainly hold true for
terrorists. In the circumstances, the change-of-address initiative seems an ineffective antiterrorist tool. Moreover, it di-
verts resources from more targeted security measures.

All Boat People Will Be Detained

Perhaps the most strained use of national security to justify immigration restrictions can be found in DOJ's treatment of
Haitian boat people. On December 14, 2001, the Bush Administration ordered that Haitians caught trying to enter the
United States be immediately detained. This represented a return to a discredited policy of detaining migrants from a particular nation in order to deter others from coming. International law disfavors detention of asylum-seekers (as many
Haitians have proven to be) and requires individual custody
decisions. In response to protests, DOJ announced that it
would resolve the inconsistency in treatment between Haitians
and other migrants by making its severe policy reward
Haitians the norm. With the exception of Cubans, INS will

now subject all undocumented migrants who have arrived by boat and have not been physically present in the United States for two years to detention and a process of expedited return. Even those found to have a "credible fear" of persecution, and could thus be legally released, will remain confined. DOJ cannot persuasively argue that indigent boat people, fleeing poverty and persecution, represent a terrorist threat. Rather, it makes the attenuated claim that the new policy will ensure that the Coast Guard focuses on its antiterror responsibilities without being diverted by detaining boat people.

These three measures hardly represent the only examples of migration policies whose efficacy as antiterror tools have been challenged. Vincent Cannistraro, the former head of counterterrorism at the Central Intelligence Agency, argues that the detention of thousands of Middle Eastern and South Asian nationals after September 11 risked "alienat[ing] the very people on whom law enforcement depends for leads." DOJ's initiative to use state and local police to enforce federal immigration laws has faced similar criticism by law enforcement officials. Undocumented immigrants will not cooperate with the police if it might result in deportation. Yet their cooperation will be crucial to homeland security.

The war on terror must be aggressive, but it must be smart. The government needs to adopt measures that reflect our core values and that meaningfully promote security. It needs to explain how its tactics achieve both goals. It should not squander its own credibility with measures that undermine our nation's guiding principles but do little to make us safer.

"Given the weaknesses in our current security system, arming pilots is the best insurance we have against another slaughter like Sept. 11."

Arming Airline Pilots Will Protect U.S. Travelers

Kathleen Parker

In the following viewpoint Kathleen Parker claims that armed pilots are the best defense against airline terrorists. Passengers put their lives in a pilot's hands when they board a plane, she argues, and therefore should not hesitate to fly with an armed pilot who can offer them protection against terrorists. Parker maintains that the threat of terrorism is so great that traditional gun control arguments do not apply. Kathleen Parker is a nationally known columnist and frequent contributor to *Jewish World Review*.

As you read, consider the following questions:

1. What was the slip-through rate at Los Angeles International Airport for government decoys carrying fake guns, according to the author?
2. What does the author insist pilots will have to do before they can carry guns on planes?
3. In Parker's opinion, why is the bill to allow pilots to carry guns not as likely to pass in the Senate?

Given the amount of energy required for thinking, and my aptitude for staring into middle space, I confess to an affection for no-brainers, such as: Should airline pilots carry guns?

Wait, wait, I'm tearing myself away from a mesmerizing galaxy of dust particles to make this public service pronouncement. Yah. Why not? Terrorists have box cutters and nefarious plans for murdering thousands by taking out helpless pilots. Here's an idea: Let's give pilots a way to defend themselves!

OK, that's a wrap. I'm exhausted. See you next week.

Would that life were so simple. Instead, during more than nine months since the savage attacks of Sept. 11 [2001], we've acted like we checked our brains curbside.

Anyone who has flown in recent months knows the drill: Little old ladies, comely blond women and [former vice president] Al Gore get frisked and searched while government decoys carrying fake guns and bombs slip through the gate 25 percent of the time, according to recent nationwide tests.

At the Los Angeles International Airport (LAX), the slip-through rate was 41 percent. LAX, you'll recall, is where Egyptian gunman Hesham Mohamed Hadayet mowed down two travelers at the El Al ticket counter on the Fourth of July [2002]. It doesn't take much of a stretch to imagine that a madman who takes a gun to an airport with a 41 percent slip-through rate could wind up on an airplane.

But not to worry; we're in safe hands. Our security folks are on top of this one: Hadayet is Egyptian; may have terrorist ties; is believed to have met with [Sept. 11 mastermind] Osama bin Laden; is a known anti-Semite, and picked a national U.S. holiday to attack people at the Israeli airline ticket counter. They'll be closing in on a motive any day now.

Let's tighten our little thinking caps a minute. Guns and bombs get through; security checkers are busy fondling the random paying (duped) customer; pilots are defenseless . . . That's not an ellipsis, but the dots that need connecting.

House of Representatives Favors Arming Pilots

Fortunately for those still forced by business or circumstance to fly, some members of the U.S. House of Representatives sharpened their pencils this week [July 15, 2002]. Wednesday, the House voted 310-113 in favor of a bill that would allow commercial pilots to sign up for an armed-pilot program.

As proposed, the program would be voluntary. Some pilots might opt out, but those comfortable with the idea of having a final shot at life—rather than being carved up by hijackers or radically deplaned by the U.S. Air Force—may take a training course and lock and load.

Arming Pilots Is Not a New Idea

Despite the concern about hypothetical risks, arming pilots is not some new experiment. About 70 percent of the pilots at major American airlines have military backgrounds, and military pilots flying outside the U.S. are required to carry handguns with them whenever they flew military planes.

Until the early 1960s, American commercial passenger pilots on any flight carrying U.S. mail were required to carry handguns. The requirement started at the beginning of commercial aviation to insure that pilots could defend the mail if their plane were to ever crash. In contrast to the current program, there were no training or screening requirements. Indeed, pilots were still allowed to carry guns until as recently as 1987. There are no records that any of these pilots (either military or commercial) carrying guns have ever caused any significant problems.

John R. Lott Jr., *National Review*, September 2, 2003.

The bill still faces the Senate, where it isn't likely to do as well owing to fierce opposition from key players combined with an uncharacteristically wimpy White House.[1] Both Transportation Secretary Norman Mineta and Homeland Security Director Tom Ridge are against arming pilots, as is John W. Magaw, head of the Transportation Security Administration.

Why? I'm not sure. Dots too small? Logic too obvious? Politics too hot? From where I sit back in coach class, nothing is hotter than a radical, Koran-chanting Islamist who thinks that killing Americans is a sacrament and that 72 virgins awaiting in heaven is a fair trade off for ramming an airplane into a tall building.

1. In 2002 the Senate passed the bill allowing airline pilots to be armed.

That's also the sort of heat a fruitcake pilot could inflict any time the mood swings. As commander of a 400-ton missile loaded with explosive fuel, a commercial pilot is already in charge of a significant lethal weapon. By inserting ourselves inside said missile, we've already put our lives into his hands. And we're worried about a gun in the cockpit?

Given a choice between trusting the screeners, whose "security measures" would get them indicted for sexual assault in any other workplace, and a trained, armed airline pilot, in whom I already have placed my trust, I'll go with the latter.

In the nightmarish event that an armed lunatic takes over my airplane, I am fundamentally not interested in handgun-control rhetoric or in slippery slope arguments that, golly, before you know it, bus drivers and train engineers and who knows who else will want guns, too. . . .

What I *am* concerned with is just one thing: stepping over a dead hijacker as I exit my safely landed airplane. Given the weaknesses in our current security system, arming pilots is the best insurance we have against another slaughter like Sept. 11. Given the obvious simplicity of this no-brainer, don't count on it.

"Armed pilots would be more inclined to go out into the cabin, whereas the primary goal should be getting the plane to the ground."

Arming Airline Pilots Will Not Protect U.S. Travelers

George Will

In the following viewpoint nationally syndicated columnist George Will supports the position taken by many airline pilots that a pilot's primary responsibility is to bring the plane and passengers safely to the ground—not engage in a gun battle with terrorists. Armed pilots, Will asserts would be more likely to go out into the cabin to face terrorists rather than stay in the cockpit and fly the plane. He points out that many pilots view the flight record of the unarmed pilots of the Israeli airline El Al—thirty-four years without a hijacking—as proof that pilots do not need to carry guns to deter terrorism.

As you read, consider the following questions:

1. Prior to the terrorist attacks of September 11, 2001, what was the policy for pilots regarding hijacking, according to Will?
2. What does the author report is a reasonable alternative to a pilot looking over his shoulder to watch for disturbances in the cabin?
3. According to Will, what is a possible reason (in addition to protection from terrorists) that the Air Line Pilots Association is in favor of arming pilots?

George Will, "Good Reasons to Keep Pilots Unarmed," www.polkonline.com, May 30, 2002. Copyright © 2002 by Washington Post Book World Service/Washington Post Writers Group. Reproduced by permission.

Three pilots of a major airline recently gathered here at George Bush Intercontinental Airport to discuss whether, as an anti-terrorism measure, pilots should be armed. The Transportation Department says guns will not be permitted in cockpits. Some in Congress will try to overturn this ban.[1] The Air Line Pilots Association [ALPA], which represents 62,000 pilots working for 42 airlines, adamantly favors arming them.

These three pilots—two trained in the military, one in civilian life—are ALPA members. They have a cumulative 75 years of experience flying for commercial airlines. None has an aversion to guns. Says one, "I was raised around guns all my life." Says another, "I've not got any affinity for gun control." Says the third, "I love guns. Been a hunter all my life. I'm adamantly against gun control."

All three oppose arming pilots. Here is why.

Arming Pilots Is a Bad Idea

They note that [the Sept. 11, 2001, terrorist attacks] triggered a reversal of assumptions. The policy for pilots regarding a hijacking had been: Don't deal with it. Before suicidal hijackers took over four planes, the procedure was for pilots to fly their aircraft to the destination the hijacker demanded.

Now, these three pilots say, the overriding priority must be to guarantee that cockpits are sealed behind bulletproof doors, protecting the flight deck from intrusion while pilots get the plane on the ground as quickly as possible. Which can be 10 minutes—as pilots know from training to deal with the problem of sudden decompression of an aircraft.

Prior to Sept. 11, if a passenger became unruly, the pilot might come back into the cabin to assert authority. No more. Says one of these three, "The flight attendants know they are on their own."

"You cannot fly an airplane and look over your shoulder, firing down the cabin," says one of these pilots. What you could do, he says, is look down the cabin by means of a closed-circuit television camera that would warn the flight

1. In 2002 Congress passed a bill allowing airline pilots to be armed.

deck of cabin disturbances requiring quick action to take the plane to the ground. Flight plans should show the nearest alternative airport at every stage of every flight.

Cowboy Pilots Are a Threat

Another potential problem with arming America's 120,000 commercial airline pilots is what one of the three pilots here calls, with no demurral from the other two, "cowboys or renegade pilots." Many commercial pilots began their flying careers as fighter pilots. Two of the three speaking here this day did. One of them says: There is some truth to the profile of fighter pilots as, well, live wires and risk-takers. Arming them might incite them to imprudent bravery. Armed pilots would be more inclined to go out into the cabin, whereas the primary goal should be getting the plane to the ground.

"The popularity of an idea does not make it a good idea," says one of these pilots, and all three, although members of ALPA, question whether the idea of arming pilots is as popular with pilots as ALPA suggests. One of these pilots was polled by phone by ALPA and considered the questions written so as to produce an expression of support for arming pilots.

There is in the airline industry the suspicion that the drive to arm pilots, to equip them for potential action back in the cabin, is for ALPA a new front in the organization's long-standing campaign to revive the requirement for a third pilot in the cockpit. The three pilots gathered here would prefer that ALPA concentrate on protecting existing jobs rather that creating new ones.

Many thoughtful pilots do favor guns as an additional layer of deterrence, and a last resort to restoring control over an aircraft before F-16s are scrambled to shoot it from the sky. Had armed pilots been flying the four planes hijacked on Sept. 11, box cutters would not have sufficed. And you do not want to know how many dangerous implements escape the detection of airport screeners while they are X-raying your shoes and frisking grandmothers to demonstrate innocence of racial or ethnic profiling.

However, the pilots of El Al, Israel's airline, are not armed, and the airline has not had a hijacking in 34 years. The three pilots consider this evidence for the argument that the deterrence effect of armed pilots is not essential. Furthermore, gunfire in the cockpit could easily shatter the windshield. In which case, says one of these pilots, "someone is going to be sucked out—the terrorist, if he's not strapped in."

"There are," says one of the three, "a lot of what-ifs and don't knows" when you decide to arm pilots. These pilots know they are against that.

> *"Biometrics is one technology that can help us achieve the goal of a safer America."*

Using Face Recognition Technology Will Make Americans Safer

John D. Woodward Jr.

Face recognition technology—a form of biometrics—compares the digital image of an individual's face to a computerized database and provides instantaneous identification. In the following viewpoint, John D. Woodward Jr. argues that using face recognition to control access to sensitive facilities at airports, prevent identity theft and fraudulent use of travel documents, and identify known or suspected terrorists can help safeguard America from terrorist attacks. He maintains further that as face recognition technology improves, it will provide even greater protection. John D. Woodward Jr., a former CIA operations officer, is a senior policy analyst at RAND, a nonprofit policy analysis and research institution.

As you read, consider the following questions:
1. What four examples of biometrics does the author argue can be used for identification purposes?
2. According to the author, how does FaceCheck work?
3. In the author's opinion, what could highly trained terrorists do to defeat facial recognition systems?

As the nation recovers from the [terrorist] attacks of September 11, 2001, we must rededicate our efforts to prevent any such terrorist acts in the future. Although terrorism can never be completely eliminated, we, as a nation, can take additional steps to counter it. We must explore many options in this endeavor. Among them, we should examine the use of emerging biometric technologies that can help improve public safety. While there is no easy, foolproof technical fix to counter terrorism, the use of biometric technologies might help make America a safer place.

"Biometrics" refers to the use of a person's physical characteristics or personal traits to identify, or verify the claimed identity of, that individual. Fingerprints, faces, voices, and handwritten signatures are all examples of characteristics that have been used to identify us in this way. Biometric-based systems provide automatic, nearly instantaneous identification of a person by converting the biometric—a fingerprint, for example—into digital form and then comparing it against a computerized database. In this way, fingerprints, faces, voices, iris and retinal images of the eye, hand geometry, and signature dynamics can now be used to identify us, or to authenticate our claimed identity, quickly and accurately. These biometric technologies may seem exotic, but their use is becoming increasingly common. In January 2000, *MIT Technology Review* named biometrics as one of the "top ten emerging technologies that will change the world." And after September 11th, biometric technologies may prove to be one of the emerging technologies that will help safeguard the nation. . . .

Controlling Access

Access control to sensitive facilities can be improved by using biometric-based identifiers. In other words, instead of identifying an individual based on something he has (a badge), or something he knows (a password or a PIN), that person will be identified based on something he *is*. For example, instead of flashing a badge, an airline worker with a need to access sensitive areas of airports could be required to present a biometric, say his iris, to a sensor. From a foot away and in a matter of seconds, this device captures the person's iris image, converts it to a *template*, or computer-readable representation, and searches a database containing the templates of authorized personnel for a match. A match confirms that the person seeking access to a particular area is in fact authorized to do so. This scenario is not science fiction. Such a system has been used at Charlotte-Douglas International Airport in North Carolina.

While not foolproof, such a biometric system is much harder to compromise than systems using a badge or badge plus PIN. As such, a biometric system to authenticate the identity of individuals seeking access to sensitive areas within airports or similar facilities represents a significant increase in security. And to the extent that terrorist acts can be thwarted by the ability to keep unauthorized individuals out of these sensitive areas, this improvement in physical security could contribute directly to a decrease in the terrorist threat.

Preventing Immigration Fraud/Identity Theft

In addition to failures to authenticate the identity of airport employees, failures to accurately identify individuals as they cross through our borders can also contribute to a terrorist attack. It is important to ensure that necessary travel documents are used only by the person to whom they were issued. Like badges and tokens, passports, visas, and boarding passes can be forged, misplaced, or stolen. While anti-fraud measures are bulk into the issuance of such documents, there is room for improvement. A biometric template of, for example, one's fingerprint (or other biometric) could be attached to the document on a bar code, chip, or magnetic strip, making it more difficult for someone to adopt a false identity or forge a travel document. To ensure security, the biometric should be encrypted and inserted into the document by a digital signature process using a trusted agent, such as a U.S. embassy's visa section.

In addition to helping prevent fraud or identity theft, we can use biometrics to make it easier for certain qualified travelers to identify themselves. For example, the Immigration and Naturalization Service (INS) currently uses biometrics in the Immigration and Naturalization Service Passenger Accelerated Service System (INSPASS). Under

INSPASS, over 45,000 international travelers, whose identities and travel papers have been vetted, have voluntarily enrolled in a system that verifies their identity at ports of entry using the biometric of hand geometry. By allowing these frequent travelers to pass through immigration quickly, INSPASS enables INS officers to devote more time and attention to problem cases.

Identifying Known or Suspected Terrorists

As the criminal investigation of the September 11th attacks appears to demonstrate, some of the terrorists were able to enter the United States using valid travel documents under their true identities, passing with little difficulty through immigration procedures at U.S. ports of entry. Once in the country, they patiently continued their planning, preparation, training, and related operational work for months and in some cases years until that fateful day. Once inside the United States, the terrorists cleverly took advantage of American freedoms to help carry out their attacks.

According to media reports, however, at least three of the suicide attackers were known to U.S. authorities as suspected terrorists. In late August 2001, the Central Intelligence Agency (CIA) passed information to the INS to be on the lookout for two men suspected of involvement in terrorist activities. The CIA apparently obtained videotape showing the men, Khalid Almihdhar and Nawaf Alhazmi, talking to people implicated in the *U.S.S. Cole* bombing. The videotape was taken in Kuala Lumpur, Malaysia, in January 2000. It is not clear when the CIA received it.

When the INS checked its database, it found that a Almihdhar and Alhazmi had successfully passed through INS procedures and had already entered the United States. The CIA asked the Federal Bureau of Investigation (FBI) to find them. But with both men already in the United States, the FBI was looking for two needles in a haystack. The FBI was still seeking the two when the hijackers struck. Khalid Almihdhar and Nawaf Alhazmi are believed to have been hijackers on American Airlines flight 77, which crashed into the Pentagon.

As the above details illustrate, we need a better way to identify individuals whom we know or suspect to be terrorists when they attempt to enter the United States. The use of biometric facial recognition is one way to make such identifications, particularly when U.S. authorities already have a photograph of the suspected terrorist whom they seek.

FaceCheck

Biometric facial recognition systems could be immediately deployed to help thwart future terrorist acts. Such a "FaceCheck" system, the term I use for the specific counterterrorism application discussed in this paper, can be done in a way that uses public safety resources effectively and efficiently and minimizes inconvenience and intrusiveness for the average traveler.

In general, facial recognition systems use a camera to capture an image of a person's face as a digital photograph. In the most common form of facial recognition, this image is manipulated and reduced to a series of numbers that represent the image in relation to the "average" face. These numbers are often referred to as a template, which is then instantly searched against a "watchlist," or computerized database of suspected terrorists' templates. This search seeks to answer the question, "Is this person in the watchlist database?" A computer-generated match or "hit" alerts the authorities to the presence of a potential threat. The value of such a system in helping to prevent individuals such as Khalid Almihdhar and Nawaf Alhazmi from entering the country is clear. Indeed, according to the *Washington Post*, a government committee appointed by Secretary of Transportation Norman Y. Mineta to review airport security measures will recommend that facial recognition systems be deployed in specified airports to improve security.

Operational Framework

Controlling access to sensitive facilities, as well as preventing immigration fraud and identity theft, can be accomplished with a variety of biometric systems. Such systems can accommodate users and are relatively easy to incorporate into current security systems (i.e., adding a digitally signed, encrypted biometric bar code to existing travel documents or badges). Moreover, the technology is readily available.

Identifying known or suspected terrorists presents a greater challenge. While fingerprint and other biometric systems could be used to identify these individuals, government authorities might find it difficult to collect the fingerprints or iris scans of suspected terrorists in order to build the database against which to compare an unknown individual. Facial recognition biometric systems, however, offer a way around this problem. Specifically, facial recognition systems will allow the identification of a suspected or known terrorist even if the only identifying information we have is a photograph. . . .

How FaceCheck Works

Although facial recognition is not a perfect technology, we should not let the perfect become the enemy of the good. The overall challenge is to make it better. Fortunately, gifted scientists and engineers are working on this challenge, and in light of the September 11th attacks, the government is likely to make additional resources available to encourage research, development, testing, and evaluation. In the meantime, we can use facial recognition operationally in a way that minimizes its weaknesses. The system works best when environmental factors such as camera angle, lighting, and facial expression are controlled to the maximum extent possible. We must apply this lesson to our operational framework.

If a person (including a terrorist) is coming to the United States from overseas, he must pass through an immigration checkpoint at the port of entry. At this checkpoint, the INS official scrutinizes the person, asks questions, and inspects the person's travel documents. The official then makes a decision as to whether the person gets into the box, i.e., enters the United States. This immigration checkpoint is one of the nation's vital first lines of defense against terrorist entry. From the perspective of counterterrorism, this checkpoint is a chokepoint where the would-be terrorist is at his most vulnerable. This is the first and probably only place in the United States where he will be closely scrutinized by trained federal officials. Here is how FaceCheck can make the checkpoint a more formidable bastion.

An individual processing through an immigration checkpoint at a port of entry should be subject to a FaceCheck whereby he would be required as part of immigration processing to pose for a photograph under completely controlled conditions. This way we minimize facial recognition's technological imperfections, which derive in large measure from attempting to use the system to find a face in a crowd. The photograph would then be processed by the facial recognition system and run against a watchlist database of suspect terrorists. If the system indicates a match, this result would be confirmed by visual inspection by the authorities, and the person could be taken to a secondary interview for heightened scrutiny.

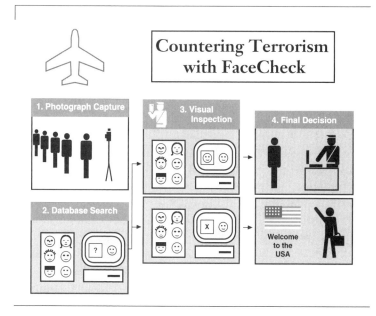

Countering Terrorism with FaceCheck

1. Photograph Capture
2. Database Search
3. Visual Inspection
4. Final Decision

Welcome to the USA

The Strategic Use of FaceCheck

Facial recognition systems do not necessarily have to be implemented to process every individual seeking to enter the United States. Rather, the authorities should use FaceCheck in a more strategic way. This would include using it randomly; in targeted ways; and in conjunction with other information. For example, FaceCheck could be run on every so many people from a given flight. It could be used at different ports of entry at different times and for different flights. Similarly, FaceCheck teams could deploy to specific ports of entry at specific times to target a specific flight in light of threat information. Testers—human guinea pigs whose images have been entered into the watchlist database—should be included in the immigration processing to rigorously evaluate the system: How well did FaceCheck do in identifying suspects?

Moreover, while we do not have to use the system on all passengers entering the United States, we should consider setting up FaceCheck stations at ports of entry and have passengers pose for photographs as though the system were in continuous use. In this way, we keep terrorists guessing as to where the systems are actually deployed or in use. We should also experiment with FaceCheck systems using closed-circuit surveillance cameras to capture images clandestinely at certain ports of entry. In this way, we can learn how well such systems work in realistic operational environments and gain information to improve their technical capabilities. Again, we do not need to inform passengers as to where such systems are actually deployed.

We also need to consider using FaceCheck for visa processing at our embassies and consulates overseas. We could easily require a visa applicant to submit to a photograph taken under controlled conditions. We could then run a search against the watchlist database. Similarly, we do not need to inform visa applicants overseas whether we are actually running FaceCheck.

Dedicated, highly trained terrorists may be able to defeat facial recognition systems. One technique may be for a terrorist to undergo cosmetic surgery to alter his facial features. As a result, he will not match his database photograph. Similarly, terrorists may try to enter the United States illegally by crossing the relatively porous borders with Canada and Mexico. But although facial recognition systems might be defeated by a surgeon's skill or an illegal border crossing, at least we force terrorists to take additional steps that drain their resources and keep them on the defensive.

Security vs. Civil Liberties

Though these facial recognition systems are not technically perfected, they are improving. There is little reason to doubt that as the technology improves, it will eventually be able to identify faces in a crowd as effectively as it currently identifies a face scanned under controlled circumstances. And while civil libertarians might decry the use of this technology as an invasion of privacy, the key lies in balancing the need for security with the need to protect civil liberties. In this regard, three brief points need to be made.

First, we do not have a constitutional right to privacy in the face we show in public. The United States Supreme Court has determined that government action constitutes a "search" when it invades a person's reasonable expectation of privacy. But the Court has found that a person does not have a reasonable expectation of privacy in those physical characteristics that are constantly exposed to the public, such as one's facial features, voice, and handwriting. Therefore, although the Fourth Amendment requires that a search conducted by government actors be "reasonable," which generally means that the individual is under suspicion, the use of facial recognition does not constitute a search. As a result, the government is not constrained, on Fourth Amendment grounds, from employing facial recognition systems in public spaces. Although the use of facial recognition may generate discussion of the desirability of enacting new regulations for the use of the technology, such use is allowed under our current legal framework.

Secondly, current legal standards recognize that we are all subject to heightened scrutiny at our borders and ports of entry. The "border exception" to the Fourth Amendment recognizes "the longstanding right of the sovereign to protect itself by stopping and examining persons and property crossing into this country." Accordingly, such searches are reasonable and do not require a warrant, probable cause, or even reasonable suspicion. When we transit our borders, therefore, the authorities can closely scrutinize our person and property in ways that they could not do in another setting. Even within our own borders, the law requires airport facilities to conduct security screening of passengers' persons and personal effects, and it is unlawful even to make jokes about threats on airport property.

Finally, it is worth noting that facial recognition systems

are not relied upon to make final determinations of a person's identity. Rather, the system alerts the authorities so that additional screening and investigation can take place. And though the system will make false matches that will subject innocent passengers to additional questioning and scrutiny, the current system routinely does the same. . . .

Biometrics Can Make America Safer

There is no high-tech silver bullet to solve the problem of terrorism. And it is doubtful that facial recognition or other biometric technologies could have prevented the terrorist attacks on September 11th. But to the extent we can improve access control at sensitive facilities such as airports, reduce identity theft and immigration fraud, and identify known or suspected terrorists, then we make terrorism more difficult in the future. Biometrics is one technology that can help us achieve the goal of a safer America.

"Face recognition is nearly useless for . . . identifying terrorists in a crowd."

Using Face Recognition Technology Will Not Make Americans Safer

Philip E. Agre

Philip E. Agre maintains in the following viewpoint that automatic face recognition technology, a form of biometrics that compares an individual's digitalized facial image to a computerized database should be banned. The potential for abuse by government and business is immense, he argues, while the benefit to the fight against terrorism is minimal. Further, Agre insists that automatic face recognition is almost useless in identifying terrorists in a crowd because it produces so many false positive matches. Philip E. Agre is a professor of information studies at the University of California, Los Angeles.

As you read, consider the following questions:
1. When does the author consider the use of automatic face recognition technology acceptable?
2. What does Agre argue will happen in countries where civil liberties hardly exist if the use of face recognition technology becomes commonplace?
3. According to the author, what measures might have prevented September 11, 2001, terrorists from boarding a plane at the Boston airport?

Given a digital image of a person's face, face recognition software matches it against a database of other images. If any of the stored images matches closely enough, the system reports the sighting to its owner. Research on automatic face recognition has been around for decades, but accelerated in the 1990s. Now it is becoming practical, and face recognition systems are being deployed on a large scale.

Some applications of automatic face recognition systems are relatively unobjectionable. Many facilities have good reasons to authenticate everyone who walks in the door, for example to regulate access to weapons, money, criminal evidence, nuclear materials, or biohazards. When a citizen has been arrested for probable cause, it is reasonable for the police to use automatic face recognition to match a mug shot of the individual against a database of mug shots of people who have been arrested previously. These uses of the technology should be publicly justified, and audits should ensure that the technology is being used only for proper purposes.

Face recognition systems in public places, however, are a matter for serious concern. The issue recently came to broad public attention when it emerged that fans attending the Super Bowl [in 2001] had unknowingly been matched against a database of alleged criminals, and when the city of Tampa [Florida] deployed a face-recognition system in the nightlife district of Ybor City. But current and proposed uses of face recognition are much more widespread. . . . The time to consider the acceptability of face recognition in public places is now, before the practice becomes entrenched and people start getting hurt.

Legal Constraints Are Minimal

Nor is the problem limited to the scattered cases that have been reported thus far. As the underlying information and communication technologies (digital cameras, image databases, processing power, and data communications) become radically cheaper over the next two decades, face recognition will become dramatically cheaper as well, even without assuming major advances in technologies such as image processing that are specific to recognizing faces. Legal constraints on the practice in the United States are minimal. (In

Europe the data protection laws will apply, providing at least some basic rights of notice and correction.) Databases of identified facial images already exist in large numbers (driver's license and employee ID records, for example), and new facial-image databases will not be hard to construct, with or without the knowledge or consent of the people whose faces are captured. (The images need to be captured under controlled conditions, but most citizens enter controlled, video-monitored spaces such as shops and offices on a regular basis.) It is nearly certain, therefore, that automatic face recognition will grow explosively and become pervasive unless action is taken now.

I believe that automatic face recognition in public places, including commercial spaces such as shopping malls that are open to the public, should be outlawed. The dangers outweigh the benefits. The necessary laws will not be passed, however, without overwhelming pressure of public opinion and organizing. To that end, this article presents the arguments against automatic face recognition in public places, followed by responses to the most common arguments in favor.

Arguments Against Automatic Face Recognition in Public Places

The potential for abuse is astronomical. Pervasive automatic face recognition could be used to track individuals wherever they go. Systems operated by different organizations could easily be networked to cooperate in tracking an individual from place to place, whether they know the person's identity or not, and they can share whatever identities they do know. This tracking information could be used for many purposes. At one end of the spectrum, the information could be leaked to criminals who want to understand a prospective victim's travel patterns. Information routinely leaks from databases of all sorts, and there is no reason to believe that tracking databases will be any different. But even more insidiously, tracking information can be used to exert social control. Individuals will be less likely to contemplate public activities that offend powerful interests if they know that their identity will be captured and relayed to anyone that wants to know.

The information from face recognition systems is easily

combined with information from other technologies. Among the many "biometric" identification technologies, face recognition requires the least cooperation from the individual. Automatic fingerprint reading, by contrast, requires an individual to press a finger against a machine. (It will eventually be possible to identify people by the DNA-bearing cells that they leave behind, but that technology is a long way from becoming ubiquitous.) Organizations that have good reasons to identify individuals should employ whatever technology has the least inherent potential for abuse, yet very few identification technologies have more potential for abuse than face recognition. Information from face recognition systems is also easily combined with so-called location technologies such as E-911 location tracking in cell phones, thus further adding to the danger of abuse.

The technology is hardly foolproof. Among the potential downsides are false positives; for example that so-and-so was "seen" on a street frequented by drug dealers. Such a report will create "facts" that the individual must explain away. Yet the conditions for image capture and recognition in most public places are far from ideal. Shadows, occlusions, reflections, and multiple uncontrolled light sources all increase the risk of false positives. As the database of facial images grows bigger, the chances of a false match to one of those images grows proportionally larger.

Face recognition is nearly useless for the application that has been most widely discussed since the September 11th [2001] attacks on New York and Washington: identifying terrorists in a crowd. As Bruce Schneier [cryptographer and biometrics expert] points out, the reasons why are statistical. Let us assume, with extreme generosity, that a face recognition system is 99.99 percent accurate. In other words, if a high-quality photograph of your face is not in the "terrorist watch list" database, then it is 99.99 percent likely that the software will not produce a match when it scans your face in real life. Then let us say that one airline passenger in ten million has their face in the database. Now, 99.99 percent probably sounds good. It means one failure in 10,000. In scanning ten million passengers, however, one failure in 10,000 means 1000 failures—and only one correct match of a real terrorist. In other words, 999 matches out of 1000 will be false, and each of those false matches will cost time and effort that could have been spent protecting security in other ways. Perhaps one would argue that 1000 false alarms are worth the benefits of one hijacking prevented. Once the initial shock of the recent attacks wears off, however, the enormous percentage of false matches will condition security workers to assume that all positive matches are mistaken. The great cost of implementing and maintaining the face recognition systems will have gone to waste. The fact is, spotting terrorists in a crowd is a needle-in-a-haystack problem, and automatic face recognition is not a needle-in-a-haystack-quality technology. Hijackings can be prevented in many ways, and resources should be invested in the measures that are likely to work.

The Public Is Poorly Informed

Many social institutions depend on the difficulty of putting names to faces without human intervention. If people could be identified just from looking in a shop window or eating in a restaurant, it would be a tremendous change in our society's conception of the human person. People would find strangers addressing them by name. Prospective customers walking into a shop could find that their credit reports and other relevant information had already been pulled up and displayed for the sales staff before they even inquire about the goods. Even aside from the privacy invasion that this represents, premature disclosure of this sort of information could affect the customer's bargaining position.

The public is poorly informed about the capabilities of the cameras that are already ubiquitous in many countries. They usually do not realize, for example, what can be done with the infrared component of the captured images. Even the phrase "face recognition" does not convey how easily the system can extract facial expressions. It is not just "identity" that can be captured, then, but data that reaches into the person's psyche. Even if the public is adequately informed about the capabilities of this year's cameras, software and data sharing can be improved almost invisibly next year.

It is very hard to provide effective notice of the presence

and capabilities of cameras in most public places, much less obtain meaningful consent. Travel through many public places, for example government offices and centralized transportation facilities, is hardly a matter of choice for any individual wishing to live in the modern world. Even in the private sector, many retail industries (groceries, for example) are highly concentrated, so that consumers have little choice but to submit to the dominant company's surveillance practices.

If face recognition technologies are pioneered in countries where civil liberties are relatively strong, it becomes more likely that they will also be deployed in countries where civil liberties hardly exist. In twenty years, at current rates of progress, it will be feasible for the Chinese government to use face recognition to track the public movements of everyone in the country.

Responses to Arguments in Favor of Automatic Face Recognition in Public Places

The civilized world has been attacked by terrorists. We have to defend ourselves. It's wartime, and we have to give up some civil liberties in order to secure ourselves against the danger.

We must certainly improve our security in many areas. I have said that myself for years. The fallacy here is in the automatic association between security and restrictions on civil liberties. Security can be improved in many ways that have no effect on civil liberties, for example by rationalizing identification systems for airport employees or training flight attendants in martial arts. Security can be improved in other ways that greatly improve privacy, for example by preventing identity theft or replacing Microsoft products with well-engineered software. And many proposals for improved security have a minimal effect on privacy relative to existing practices, for example searching passengers' luggage properly. The "trade-off" between security and civil liberties, therefore, is over-rated, and I am surprised by the speed with which many defenders of freedom have given up any effort to defend the core value of our society as a result of the terrorist attack.

Once we transcend automatic associations, we can think clearly about the choices that face us. We should redesign our security arrangements to protect both security and civil liberties. Among the many security measures we might choose, it seems doubtful that we would choose the ones that, like automatic face recognition in public places, carry astronomical dangers for privacy. At least any argument for such technologies requires a high standard of proof.

But the case for face recognition is straightforward. They were looking for two of the terrorists and had photographs of them. Face recognition systems in airports would have caught them.

I'm not sure we really know that the authorities had photographs that were good enough for face recognition, even for those small number of suspects that they claim to have placed on a terrorist watch list. But even if we grant the premise, not much follows from it. First, the fact that the authorities suspected only two of the nineteen hijackers reminds us that automatic face recognition cannot recognize a face until it is in the database. Most hijackers are not on lists of suspected terrorists, and even if those particular hijackers had been prevented from boarding their planes, seventeen others would have boarded.

Shoddy Security Procedures

More importantly, security procedures at the Boston airport and elsewhere were so shoddy, on so many fronts, that a wide variety of improvements would have prevented the hijackings. If you read the white paper about the hijackings from the leading face-recognition company, Visionics, it becomes clear that face recognition is really being suggested to plug holes in identification systems. Terrorist watch lists include the terrorists' names, and so automatic face recognition is only necessary in those cases where the government possesses high-quality facial photographs of terrorists but does not know their names (not very common) or where the terrorists carry falsified identification cards in names that the government does not know. In fact, some of the terrorists in the recent attacks appear to have stolen identities from innocent people. The best solution to this problem is to repair the immensely destructive weaknesses in identification procedures, for example at state DMV's, that have been widely publicized for at least fifteen years. If these recent attacks do not motivate us to fix our identity systems, then we are truly lost. But if we do fix them, then the role that automatic face recognition actually plays in the context of other security measures becomes quite marginal.

Biometric Technology Can Be a Threat

Biometric technologies can clearly threaten our liberties. . . . Not many want to be tracked by the authorities, or treated like human bar code just because technology has made that easy. Possible applications of biometric technologies range from an involuntary "everybody included" database—exemplified by the calls today for a government-required national ID card—to privately owned and managed "members only" biometric systems that contain data only on individuals who have garnered clearance for a particular private application. Political liberty is threatened by involuntary, government-mandated databases but not by private applications as long as government and private data are kept separate. Policymakers must recognize the relevant distinctions to make rational policy decisions with respect to the inevitable public and private use of biometric identification systems in the years to come.

Clyde Wayne Crews Jr., *Cato Policy Analysis*, Cato Institute, September 17, 2002.

That said, from a civil liberties perspective we ought to distinguish among different applications of face recognition. Those applications can be arranged along a spectrum. At one end of the spectrum are applications in public places, for example scanning crowds in shops or on city streets. Those are the applications that I propose banning. At the other end of the spectrum are applications that are strongly bounded by legal due process, for example matching a mug shot of an arrested person to a database of mug shots of people who have been arrested in the past. When we consider any applications of automatic face recognition, we ought to weigh the dangers to civil liberties against the benefits. In the case of airport security, the proposed applications fall at various points along the spectrum. Applications that scan crowds in an airport terminal lie toward the "public" end of the spectrum; applications that check the validity of a boarding passenger's photo-ID card by comparing it with the photo that is associated with that card in a database lies toward the "due process" end of the spectrum. The dangers of face scanning in public places (e.g., the tracking of potentially unbounded categories of individuals) may not apply to applications at the "due process" end of the scale. It is important, therefore, to evaluate proposed systems in their specifics, and not in terms of abstract slogans about the need for security. . . .

A Civil Liberties Threat

Your arguments are scare tactics. Rather than trying to scare people with scenarios about slippery slopes, why don't you join in the constructive work of figuring out how the systems can be used responsibly?

The arguments in favor of automatic face recognition in public places are "scare tactics" too, in that they appeal to our fear of terrorism. But some fears are justified, and it is reasonable to talk about them. Terrorism is a justifiable fear, and so is repression by a government that is given too much power. History is replete with examples of both. Plenty of precedents exist to suppose that automatic face recognition, once implemented and institutionalized, will be applied to ever-broader purposes. The concern about slippery slopes is not mere speculation, but is based on the very real politics of all of the many issues to which automatic face recognition could be applied. My argument here *is* intended to contribute to the constructive work of deciding how automatic face recognition can be responsibly used. It can be responsibly used in contexts where the individuals involved have been provided with due process protections, and it cannot be responsibly used in public places. I fully recognize that literally banning automatic face recognition in public places is a major step. The reason to ban it, though, is simple: the civil liberties dangers associated with automatic face recognition are virtually in a class by themselves.

Liberty is not absolute. It is reasonable for the government to curtail liberty to a reasonable degree for the sake of the collective good.

Certainly so. The question is which curtailments of liberty provide benefits that are worth the danger. The argument here is simply that automatic face recognition in public places does not meet that test. . . .

What do you have to hide?

This line is used against nearly every attempt to protect personal privacy, and the response in each case is the same. People have lots of valid reasons, personal safety for example, to prevent particular others from knowing particular information about them. Democracy only works if groups can organize and develop their political strategies in seclusion from the government and from any established interests they might be opposing. This includes, for example, the identities of people who might travel through public places to gather for a private political meeting. In its normal use, the question "What do you have to hide?" stigmatizes all personal autonomy as anti-social. As such it is an authoritarian demand, and has no place in a free society.

Periodical Bibliography

The following articles have been selected to supplement the diverse views presented in this chapter.

American Civil Liberties Union — "Q&A on the Pentagon's 'Total Information Awareness' Program," April 20, 2003. www.aclu.org.

Alberto Baldeo and Annan Boodram — "Immigration & Terrorism: The U.S. Responds to Attacks," *Caribbean Voice*, October 2001. www.caribvoice.org.

David Carr — "The Futility of Homeland Defense," *Atlantic Monthly*, January 2002. www.theatlantic.com.

Dan Caterinicchia — "DARPA Developing Info Awareness," *Federal Computer Week*, October 17, 2002. www.fcw.com.

Council on Foreign Relations — "Terrorism: Q&A," 2003. www.terrorismanswers.com.

G. Russell Evans — "Runaway Immigration Begets Terrorism," *Americanism Educational League*, November 7, 2001. www.americanism.org.

Mark Krikorian — "Safety in (Lower) Numbers: Immigration and Homeland Security," *Center for Immigration Studies*, October 2002. www.cis.org.

James G. Lakely — "Closing Immigration Loopholes Is the First Step in Fighting Terrorism," *Free Lance-Star*, October 7, 2001. www.fredericksburg.com.

Nancy Cook Lauer — "Tighter Borders May Put State in Bind: Some Worried Stricter Regulations Will Stifle Tourism," *Tallahassee Democrat*, June 17, 2002. www.tallahassee.com.

Diana Lynne — "Immigration Aiding, Abetting Terrorism: New Study Fuels Open-Border Versus Restrictionist Debate," *WorldNet Daily*, May 22, 2002. www.worldnetdaily.com.

Tanya Metaksa — "Arming Pilots: A Vote Against Terrorism," *Front Page Magazine*, July 17, 2002. www.frontpagemag.com

Pittsburgh Post-Gazette — "Security First: Slow the Rush to Arm American Pilots," August 29, 2003. www.post-gazette.com.

John Poindexter	"Overview of the Information Awareness Office, Defense Advanced Research Projects Agency (DARPA)," DARPATech 2002 Conference speech, August 2, 2002. www.fas.org.
William Safire	"You Are a Suspect," *New York Times*, November 14, 2002.
Salon.com News	"Grave Questions of Invasion of Privacy," November 26, 2002. www.salon.com.
Washington Post	"Total Information Awareness," November 16, 2002.

CHAPTER 4

How Is the U.S. War on Terrorism Affecting the World?

Chapter Preface

"The illegal drug trade is the financial engine that fuels many terrorist organizations around the world," then–speaker of the house Dennis Hastert said in September 2001—less than two weeks after the terrorist attacks on the United States—as he announced the formation of a new task force to combat drug trafficking. Because of the international scope of terrorism and illegal drug trafficking, America's struggles against both have worldwide ramifications. While politicians, terrorism experts, and drug policy experts all agree with Hastert's assertion that illegal drugs are a primary funding source for terrorism, they disagree on the role the U.S. drug war plays in this international scenario. Some, like Hastert, argue that the war on drugs must be stepped up to help staunch the flow of drug money to terrorism.

With this goal in mind, Attorney General John Ashcroft is supporting new legislation that would expand the Justice Department's USA PATRIOT Act. The Vital Interdiction of Criminal Terrorists Organizations (VICTORY) Act includes extra penalties for drug dealers alleged to be linked to terrorist groups and increases the government's power to seize records and property and conduct wiretaps in connection with "narcoterrorism" investigations. The VICTORY Act was introduced in the fall 2003 session of Congress, and as of February 2004, is still in committee.

Linking domestic drug use to terrorism is also part of the expanded war on drugs. During the 2002 Super Bowl, the Office of National Drug Control Policy launched an aggressive $3.5 million ad campaign that emphasized the link between illegal drugs and terrorism, and characterized drug users as terrorist financiers. One ad asked viewers, "Where do terrorists get their money?" The answer: "If you buy drugs, some of it might come from you."

However, many commentators maintain that it is America's decades-long drug war that makes drug trafficking so lucrative for terrorist organizations. Making drugs illegal and difficult to obtain drives up the price of drugs, they point out, without reducing demand. Ending the war on drugs, they contend, is the best way to eliminate the illegal drug trade that helps support terrorism. According to Kevin B. Zeese, president of the advocacy group Common Sense for Drug Policy, changing U.S. drug laws so that they emphasize treatment and prevention of drug abuse combined with a government-controlled drug market for medically approved opium-based drugs would help stop the international drug trafficking that supports terrorism. Zeese argues that "once we realize that the cause of this crime cash flow is the drug laws . . . we can recognize that with a stroke of a pen, we can change the laws and take away a major source of terrorist funding."

Experts agree that illegal drug trafficking funds international terrorism although they are divided on whether the U.S. war on drugs is helping to solve or exacerbating the problem. Authors in the following chapter look closely at the extent of worldwide terrorist activity, and the effect of U.S. terrorism policies on Israel and the United Nations, as they explore the global effect of the U.S. war on terrorism.

*"2002 saw . . . a significant decrease in the
number of terrorist attacks, from 355 in
2001, down to 199 in 2002."*

The U.S. War on Terrorism Has Caused a Decrease in Worldwide Terrorism

Colin L. Powell

U.S. secretary of state Colin L. Powell argues in the following viewpoint that the war on terrorism, while far from won, is being successfully waged. Statistics showing a decrease in the number of terrorist attacks worldwide from 2001 to 2002 are proof of that success he maintains. Moreover, the liberation of Afghanistan and Iraq by American-led forces has resulted in a reduction of terrorism in those countries and around the world. Powell insists that terrorists are being increasingly isolated by the seizure of their financial assets and the diplomatic and military pressure put on countries that provide aid to them.

As you read, consider the following questions:
1. What is the effect of UN sanctions on terrorists, in the author's opinion?
2. Why does Powell argue that the liberation of Iraq is a great victory for freedom?
3. According to the author, how many Americans perished as a result of terrorism in 2002?

Colin L. Powell, televised address, Washington, DC, April 30, 2003.

The international campaign against terrorism that President [George W.] Bush launched and leads continues to be waged on every continent. With every passing month, that campaign has intensified.

As the President has pledged, "With the help of a broad coalition, we will make certain that terrorists and their supporters are not safe in any corner or cave of the world."

I am pleased to report that unprecedented progress has been made across the international community. Nations everywhere now recognize that we are all in this together; none of us can combat terrorism alone. This global threat demands a global response. Concerted action is essential, and together we are taking that concerted action.

Countries across the globe have taken concrete antiterrorism steps, the kinds of steps called for in the pathbreaking United Nations Security Council Resolution 1373. The world's regional organizations have followed suit with reinforcing measures. United Nations sanctions have been imposed on many terrorist groups and on individuals, officially making these groups and individuals international pariahs.

And here in the United States, we have designated additional groups and Foreign Terrorist Organizations. We and other members of the international community are sharing intelligence and law enforcement information and cooperating more closely than ever before, and we are working with our partners around the world to help them build their domestic capacities to combat the terrorist threat within and across their national boundaries.

Our own capacity to combat terrorism has been strengthened by the establishment of the Department of Homeland Security under the very, very able leadership and direction of Governor Tom Ridge.

As a result of all of these efforts, thousands of terrorists have been captured and detained. For those still at large, life has definitely become more difficult. It is harder for terrorists to hide and find safe haven. It is harder for them to organize and sustain operations. Terrorist cells have been broken up, networks disrupted, and plots foiled.

The financial bloodlines of terrorist organizations have been severed. Since [the September 11, 2001, terrorist attacks on the United States], more than $134 million of terrorist assets have been frozen. All around the world, countries have been tightening their border security and better safeguarding their critical infrastructures, both physical infrastructures and virtual infrastructures.

Terrorists Are Becoming Isolated

States that sponsor terrorism are under international pressure and increasingly isolated. Much of this life-saving work has gone on behind the scenes. Meanwhile, U.S.-led coalition forces destroyed a major terrorist stronghold in Afghanistan. In the process, they liberated the Afghan people from the dual tyranny of the [ruling] Taliban and [the terrorist group] al Qaida.

So too, the liberation of Iraq is a great victory for freedom. It has freed the international community from the threat posed by the potentially catastrophic combination of a rogue regime, weapons of mass destruction and terrorists. And it has freed the Iraqi people from a vicious oppressor.

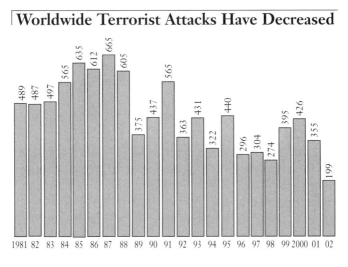

Worldwide Terrorist Attacks Have Decreased

"Patterns of Global Terrorism—2002," Department of State Publication 11038, Office of the Coordinator for Counterterrorism, April 30, 2003.

Now, we and our coalition partners are committed to helping the liberated Iraqi people. They deserve and will get a stable and united country under a representative government. Now, Iraq's great natural talent and wealth will be used to benefit all of its citizens.

To the region and the world, Iraq can become an example of a state transformed. Instead of a threat to international peace and security, it can now become a contributor to regional and international peace and security.

These are all remarkable achievements, but terrorism still casts its grim shadow across the globe. The international campaign against terrorism must press forward on every front diplomatic, intelligence, law enforcement, financial and military. As our report [Patterns of Global Terrorism—2002] indicates, 2002 saw an increase, in global resolve and effectiveness against terrorism and a significant decrease in the number of terrorist attacks, from 355 in 2001, down to 199 in 2002.

That said, last year [2002] terrorist attacks occurred in every region of the world. The terrorist bombings in Bali last October [2002] killed some 200 people from two dozen different countries. That same month, terrorists took 800 people hostage in a Moscow theater, the largest terrorist kidnapping ever. Terrorists also struck in Mombassa, killing 15 people in a hotel, while attempting to murder many more by firing a missile at a commercial airliner. Of the 725 people who perished as a result of terrorism in 2002, 30 were United States citizens, several of them members of our State Department family.

Even as I speak, terrorists are planning appalling crimes and trying to get their hands on weapons of mass destruction. We cannot and will not relax our resolve, our efforts and our vigilance. We hope that this report will increase public awareness of the historic efforts that we and our partners are making to combat terrorism and to safeguard our citizens against terrorism.

*"Occupied Iraq has become the exporter
and inspiration of terrorism to neighboring
countries and beyond."*

The U.S. War on Terrorism Has Caused an Increase in Worldwide Terrorism

Georgie Anne Geyer

In 2003 the United States led a coalition to depose Iraqi leader Saddam Hussein, whom the Bush administration accused of helping terrorists. The war was part of America's larger war on terrorism. The U.S. war in Iraq has caused an increase in terrorist activity in that country, which has spilled over into neighboring nations such as Turkey, Georgie Anne Geyer claims in the following viewpoint. Rather than reducing terrorism, she maintains, America's poorly planned occupation of Iraq is encouraging it. She argues that the American occupation has destroyed the existing Iraqi political and military infrastructure and not replaced it with anything viable. Thus, she maintains, Iraqis are at the mercy of guerrillas fighting the coalition troops and are increasingly vulnerable to terrorist recruitment. Georgie Anne Geyer is a nationally syndicated columnist.

As you read, consider the following questions:

1. What do American war planners think will mark the end of the war in Iraq, in Geyer's opinion?
2. How does the United States view Iraq in terms of the war on terrorism, in the author's opinion?
3. What is "fourth-generation warfare," according to the author?

Georgie Anne Geyer, "Iraq War Is Spawning Terrorism, Anti-Americanism in Islamic World," *Columbus Dispatch*, December 7, 2003, p. B-5. Copyright © 2003 by *Columbus Dispatch*. Reproduced by permission of Universal Press Syndicate.

A merican war planners believe they are managing a con-flict that is largely contained within Iraq,[1] one that will end when we have defeated a finite number of enemy com-batants there. They also think we are drawing into Iraq for-eign terrorists whose cause can be defeated there.

But more and more evidence, as many of us feared, indi-cates that instead the flow is going the other way—that oc-cupied Iraq has become the exporter and inspiration of ter-rorism to neighboring countries and beyond.

Take the recent [November 2003] bombings in Istanbul of the Jewish synagogues and the British consulate general and bank. At first, it was reasonable to speculate that the acts were a continuation of the Internal Kurdish terrorism that has so long rent Turkey. But the Turkish government has clearly said no; these violent truck bombings were indeed re-lated to [the terrorist group] al-Qaida, and most of the ter-rorists involved in the attacks had traveled at some time to Afghanistan, Pakistan or Iran for training.

Turkey—an Extension of the War in Iraq

Moreover, CNN reported in [December 2003] from Turk-ish intelligence agency sources that they considered the at-tacks "an extension of the war in Iraq into Turkey."

Those sources also said there has been a proliferation of weapons being smuggled from Iraq into neighboring coun-tries such as Jordan, Saudi Arabia and Turkey, including surface-to-air missiles that could be used against airliners in those countries.

The American position on the war has been that Iraq is "the front line in the war against terrorism," but the real configuration of the struggle is far more diffuse and compli-cated. A front line presupposes a traditional war in which en-emies face one another and one side will eventually vanquish the other; but the war in Iraq takes on a more cellular struc-ture, in which cells form, re-form, break up and then re-form again, often in protective coloring.

Even a bloody confrontation like the one this week [De-

---

1. In 2003 the United States led a coalition to oust Iraqi leader Saddam Hussein, whom Bush administration officials accused of helping terrorists.

cember 2, 2003] in Samarra, where highly armed and mobilized American troops defeated an Iraqi enemy that came out into the open more than ever before, does not disprove these observations. In the aftermath of Samarra, journalists and other observers were told by Iraqis that the mission had only created more anti-Americanism.

War in Iraq Inspires Terrorists

[Youssef] Choueiri [of the University of Exeter's Institute of Arab and Islamic Studies in England] said that, far from defeating terrorism, America's military involvement in Iraq and Afghanistan [to topple regimes thought to aid terrorists]—and what appears to be the failure of U.S. forces to establish nationwide stability in either country—may be inspiring terrorist groups.

"The result of this is actually a clear indication to all these groups that America does not have a clear strategy beyond using brute force, and the reaction to this is an increase in terrorism rather than a decrease in terrorist attacks," Choueiri said. "And we've seen this in Indonesia, in the Philippines, across the Middle East, as well as in Europe itself. That is, terrorist attacks, operations—even aborted ones—have actually increased, despite the increase in security measures and other policy decisions which were made to curb terrorism."

Jeremy Bransten, *Radio Free Europe/Radio Liberty*, September 12, 2003. www.rferl.org.

The real danger is that Iraq, rather than being the cemetery for terrorism, has become, as those of us who know the area long predicted, the incubator of it. There had been no al-Qaida-linked terrorism in Turkey before these attacks; if you look around the world, you see either Islamic fundamentalist or al-Qaida gains in political contests, whether in Pakistan, Malaysia, Jordan or Kuwait. Anti-Americanism is peaking in the Islamic world.

Meanwhile, inside Iraq, the political situation seems as far from solution as ever. . . . The Bush administration thought it had the answer—handing over power to the Iraqis through councils the American coalition would nominate and control. But the Ayatollah Ali al-Sistani, the senior Shiite cleric in the country, bollixed the whole plan (people in occupied nations seem to figure out quickly how to sabotage the confident oc-cupiers) by issuing a *fatwa* saying that any new government must be the result of direct elections. This would give the majority Shiites the power they have long wanted.

In Iraq, the enemy combatants' patterns of attack are in-creasingly clear. They have moved; as if following a guerrilla warfare handbook, from attacks on coalition military targets, to attacks on coalition-friendly foreign governments such as Italy and Spain, to attacks on humanitarian institutions, such as the United Nations, to attacks on Iraqis who are working with the invaders to warn against "collaboration."

Each step tries to destroy another arm of the occupation. And the attacks are increasing, with American deaths in [De-cember 2003] double those of previous months.

Some of our best analysts are becoming concerned that, no matter what the United States or anyone else does now, the Iraq state simply cannot be reconstituted. This has noth-ing to do with how awful [Iraqi leader] Saddam Hussein's state was, but everything to do with the fact that we have broken down the structures that did exist in a country of tor-tuous differences and unleashed the destructive dogs of guerrilla war, often called "fourth-generation warfare."

"In Iraq," military historian William Lind says, "the two fatal early errors were outlawing the Baath Party and dis-banding the Iraqi army. Outlawing the Baath deprived the Sunni community of its only political vehicle, which meant it had no choice but to fight us. Disbanding the Iraqi army left us with no native force that could maintain order and also provided the resistance with a large pool of armed and trained fighters.

"We fought to destroy two regimes, but what we ended up doing was destroying two states. Neither in Afghanistan[2] nor in Iraq are we able to re-create the state, which means that fourth-generation, nonstate forces will come to dominate both places. "And," he summed up, "neither we nor any other state knows how to defeat fourth-generation enemies."

2. In fall 2001 the United States went to war in Afghanistan to oust the ruling Tal-iban, whom the Bush administration claimed had given safe harbor to the terrorist organization responsible for the September 11, 2001, terrorist attacks.

> *"We reversed our policy of appeasement after September 11 and began defending ourselves [against terrorists] with force, [so] we should allow and encourage Israel to defend itself with force."*

The U.S. War on Terrorism Undermines the Israeli War on Terrorism

Andrew Bernstein

The United States fights terrorism globally but refuses to do anything about Palestinian terrorism against Israel, Andrew Bernstein insists in the following viewpoint. The United States must stop demanding that Israel negotiate with the Palestine Liberation Organization, he argues. Instead, Bernstein maintains, the United States should encourage Israel—the lone democracy in the Middle East—to aggressively defend itself by eliminating PLO leader Yasir Arafat. Andrew Bernstein is a senior writer for the Ayn Rand Institute.

As you read, consider the following questions:
1. According to Bernstein, why does the Bush administration oppose Israel's elimination of Yasir Arafat?
2. In which city does the author report that the Israelis had Arafat and the PLO surrounded in 1982?
3. In Bernstein's opinion, what is under attack by terrorist organizations in addition to the United States and Israel?

Andrew Bernstein, "The U.S. Must Stop Undermining Israel's War on Terrorism," *Media Link*, September 23, 2003. Copyright © 2003 by Ayn Rand® Institute. All rights reserved. Reproduced by permission.

President [George W.] Bush acknowledges that [Palestinian leader] Yasser Arafat has "failed as a leader" and recognizes that his promises to fight terrorism are nothing but empty lies. So why does his administration oppose Arafat's elimination? If [terrorist] Bin Laden or [Iraqi leader] Saddam Hussein were holed up in a compound surrounded by U.S. troops, is there any doubt as to what the outcome would be? Why is Arafat different?

The answer is that the Bush administration continues to uphold the absurd contradiction of appeasing Palestinian terrorism while supposedly fighting the broader phenomenon of Islamic terrorism elsewhere in the world. According to [U.S. secretary of state] Colin Powell, the result of Arafat's removal would be "rage throughout the Arab world, the Muslim world, and in many other parts of the world." But where is the rage—in this case a morally justified rage—of Mr. Powell and the U.S. government toward the terrorists who repeatedly murder Israeli civilians?

America has failed to learn the full lesson of September 11, 2001 [when Arab terrorists attacked the United States]: that appeasement only invites more and worse attacks. The atrocities of that day were merely the most egregious attacks against us by Islamic terrorists. They had kidnapped our diplomats in Teheran, murdered U.S. servicemen in Lebanon and Saudi Arabia, bombed our embassies in Kenya and Tanzania, attacked the *U.S.S. Cole* in Yemen—and for more than two decades we did nothing to defend ourselves. For the same reason that we reversed our policy of appeasement after September 11 and began defending ourselves with force, we should allow and encourage Israel to defend itself with force.

For years the U.S. government has pressured Israel into suicidal negotiations with Palestinian terrorists. Israel had Arafat and the PLO [Palestine Liberation Organization] surrounded south of Beirut in 1982, and was ready to eradicate them, but was restrained by President [Ronald] Reagan, who pressured the Israelis to allow Arafat and his organization safe passage to Tunisia. Despite the price paid in blood by innocent Israelis and Americans since, and despite Arafat's empty promises to fight Palestinian terrorism, the Bush administration continues to urge Israel to keep its troops out of the West Bank and to exercise "restraint."

For several compelling reasons the United States must desist from restraining Israel. The death of Arafat and the destruction of murderous groups like Hamas and Hizbollah will eliminate terrorists who hate the United States. It will strengthen Israel, our sole ally in the area, who will no longer have to live with constant suicide attacks. And the demise of Palestinian terrorism will prevent the creation of a Palestinian state, which given the hostility to the West of Palestinian leaders, would only add another independent nation to those already supporting terrorism.

"I'm tying your hands for a good cause, Prime Minister Sharon . . ."

Lurie. © 2001 by Cartoonews International Syndicate, N.Y.C., USA. Reproduced by permission.

There are also deeper moral reasons for setting Israel free to defend itself. The U.S. government needs to understand that more than Israel and America is under attack by terrorist organizations and regimes: Western Civilization is. At its deepest level, this is a struggle between two philosophies and two civilizations. Our murderous and tyrannical enemies are morally committed to their anti-Western ideology. Are we committed to our ideology? The terrorists know of our overwhelming military might—but they sense, too, our vacillating moral weakness. The U.S. government must fight this war in the name of the right and supremacy of Western Civilization, a culture vastly superior to Islamic culture in its ability to promote man's life on earth.

Israel is the lone country in the Middle East that stands for freedom, individual rights, secularism, reason, science and prosperity. Every Arab government is a dictatorship—be it a monarchy, theocracy or military state. Only in Israel is there freedom of speech and of the press, freedom of religion and the right to private property. The honest, nonviolent Arab living in Israel enjoys far greater freedom than he would under any Arab regime, including Arafat's. Israel, as the sole Western nation in that region, must be encouraged to apply its military superiority to achieve victory over the terrorists.

Urging the Israelis to destroy Arafat and to fight terrorists aggressively is good for the United States, both militarily and morally. We will then have an effective, trustworthy ally fighting by our side. More important, it will show the world that we are committed to the values of Western Civilization, that we will defend them to our last breath, and that we will not yield. Such uncompromising commitment to freedom and to Western values is a weapon far more powerful than any in our military arsenal.

> *"In America's war against terrorism, it is imperative that America distinguish friend from foe, good from evil, the opponents of terrorism from the perpetrators."*

The U.S. War on Terrorism Supports the Israeli War on Terrorism

Impact

The editors of *Impact* argue in the following viewpoint that as America's most trusted and reliable moral and military ally in the Middle East, Israel must be able to depend on support from the United States to fight terrorists in its own country. Further, the editors maintain that U.S. support of Israel is vital to America; if Israel is destroyed, terrorists will be able to turn their full attention to the destruction of the United States. *Impact* is the newsletter of the Ayn Rand Institute, an intellectual organization that promotes reason, individualism, and freedom.

As you read, consider the following questions:
1. Why do the editors of *Impact* maintain that Israel and its attackers are not moral equals?
2. According to the editors, why is Israel the target of terrorist organizations?
3. In the editors' opinion, what should America's position be regarding Israel's fight against terrorism?

We hold that the state of Israel has a moral right to exist and to defend itself against attack—and that the United States should unequivocally support Israel. On television, on radio, in newspapers, on college campuses—throughout our culture, the Ayn Rand Institute (ARI) has been defending the use of retaliatory force against terrorists. This ad hoc publication outlines our position and illustrates the impact of our intellectual activism.

We stand for individual rights and freedom. In the name of justice, of defending the good, we support Israel. In a region dominated by despotism and totalitarian dictatorships, Israel alone upholds rights. Defending Israel—our only true ally in the Mideast—is in America's own self-interest.

No Moral Equality Between Israel and Its Enemies

Israel and those who attack it are not moral equals. Israel is a free, Westernized country, which recognizes the individual rights of its citizens (such as their right to property and freedom of speech). It uses military force only in self-defense, in order to protect itself.

Those attacking Israel, by contrast, are terrorist organizations, theocracies, dictatorships and would-be dictators. They do not recognize the individual rights of their own subjects, much less those of the citizens of Israel. They initiate force indiscriminately in order to retain and expand their power. In contrast to the state of Israel, such organizations and regimes have no moral right to exist.

Israel Attacked for Its Virtues

Fundamentally, Israel is the target of these organizations and regimes precisely because of its virtues: it is an oasis of freedom and prosperity in a desert of tyranny and stagnation. If Israel is destroyed, the enemies of freedom attacking it will be able to turn their full attention to the United States. The United States must not let this happen.

Israel's War Is America's War

In America's war against terrorism, it is imperative that America distinguish friend from foe, good from evil, the op-

The Israeli-Palestinian Conflict May Impede the War on Terrorism

Could the current crisis between Israelis and Palestinians hurt the U.S.-led campaign against terrorism?

Yes, experts say. The Bush administration will find it harder to win support in the Arab world for continued moves against the al-Qaeda terrorist network and future steps against Iraq if its efforts take place against a backdrop of Israeli-Palestinian bloodshed. But there's no easy way to stop the violence, which is taking place in the context of one of the world's most protracted conflicts.

What is the Israeli-Palestinian conflict about?

Experts describe the conflict as a struggle between two rival national movements—one Jewish, one Arab—over the sliver of land between the Jordan River and the Mediterranean Sea. The first clashes of the current crisis erupted on September 29, 2000, when a Palestinian *intifada* (Arabic for "uprising") began in the wake of a failed peace summit at Camp David and a controversial walk by then Israeli opposition leader Ariel Sharon to a Jerusalem site sacred to both sides. Israeli leaders say Palestinian leader Yasir Arafat broke a series of 1990s peace pacts, used violence as a political tool, and deliberately resorted to terrorism after spurning a generous Israeli proposal at Camp David; Palestinian leaders say Israel never made a just peace offer and continues to besiege them, illegally occupy the West Bank and Gaza Strip, and confiscate Palestinian land for Jewish settlements.

Council on Foreign Relations, 2003.

ponents of terrorism from the perpetrators. In the name of justice and self-preservation, therefore, America should uncompromisingly encourage and support Israel in the common fight against the enemies of freedom.

"[The United Nations] was basically useless during the biggest struggle of its existence, the Cold War, and may prove to be equally so in the war on terrorism."

The U.S. War on Terrorism Has Made the United Nations Irrelevant

W. James Antle III

In 2003 the United States led a coalition to depose Iraqi leader Saddam Hussein, whom the Bush administration accused of aiding terrorists. The Iraq war was part of America's larger war against terrorism. In the following viewpoint W. James Antle III contends that UN refusal to condone force in Iraq has rendered it irrelevant in solving the complex international conflicts of the twenty-first century. Conservatives have long been calling for lesser involvement or a complete end to American participation in the United Nations because its policies are often in conflict with American interests, he claims. The United Nations and other international organizations like it have outlived their usefulness and should be disbanded. W. James Antle III is a primary columnist for IntellectualConservative.com.

As you read, consider the following questions:
1. What terms are used to justify the war in Iraq, according to Antle?
2. In the author's opinion, why do conservatives oppose the United Nations?

W. James Antle III, "U.N. May Be a Casualty of the Iraq War," www. IntellectualConservative.com, March 26, 2003. Copyright © 2003 by IntellectualConservative.com. Reproduced by permission.

Before the first shot was fired in the war with Iraq,[1] one hapless bystander was wounded, perhaps mortally. This war may yet be the beginning of the end for the United Nations.

In his St. Patrick's Day speech outlining his ultimatum for [Iraqi leader] Saddam Hussein, President George W. Bush listed the U.N. Security Council's unwillingness to enforce its own resolutions as part of the rationale for American military action. Even before this speech, the president warned that failure to support the use of force in the face of Iraqi defiance would make the U.N. "irrelevant." Now the Security Council's position on the war and the opposition of permanent members France, Russia and China has proved itself incapable of preventing a coalition led by the United States and Great Britain from waging war for regime change in Iraq.

Conservatives of all stripes have long been critical of the United Nations, but support for getting "the U.S. out of the U.N." has generally been limited to smaller conservative groups and harder-line proponents of constitutionalism and American sovereignty. Calls for ending American membership in the U.N. have generally been dismissed as the conspiratorial locutions of the "black helicopter set." Legislation regularly filed by Representative Ron Paul (R-Tex.) to withdraw the U.S. from the world body has generally gone nowhere and met with little support even among conservative Republicans.

End U.S. Involvement in the U.N.

Yet in the last week [March 26, 2003], there has been open speculation that the U.N.'s days were numbered and arguments for ending or at least cutting back the U.S.'s role from well-known commentators who are generally favorable toward internationalism. Writing in the *Wall Street Journal*, Joshua Muravchik argued against "a presumption that Security Council approval is the necessary prerequisite for the use of American force abroad." Richard Perle wrote in *The Guardian* that the Iraq war will refute "the fantasy of the U.N.

---

1. In 2003 the United States led a coalition to oust Iraqi leader Saddam Hussein, whom the Bush administration accused of aiding terrorists. The Iraq war was part of America's larger war against terrorism.

as the foundation of a new world order," by demonstrating "coalitions of the willing" to be "the true alternative to the anarchy of the abject failure of the U.N." Calls for ending or curtailing U.S. involvement in the U.N. came from Charles Krauthammer, Mona Charen, William Kristol, Linda Chavez and David Gerlernter. These are not [ultraconservative John] Birchers; they are mainstream pundits.

The UN Is an Obstructionist Body

Fortunately the UN's role is undergoing widespread scrutiny in the wake of Iraq's joyous liberation [by the United States in 2003] which occurred despite the organization's best efforts to prevent it. It may be past time to acknowledge that while the United Nations is a good idea in theory, in practice it has evolved in to obstructionist body whose demise is overdue.

Steve Fantina, *American Daily*, April 11, 2003.

Indeed, during the [1993] Gulf War the air was full of happy talk about the U.N.'s productive role and the establishment of a New World Order. Some of that kind of rhetoric still persists, but mainly this war has been justified in terms of stark national security interests. In defiance of a pseudo-governmental U.N., the U.S. professes to be acting in defense of these interests with the help of allied countries who chose to go along.

At the very least, conservatives appear to be moving toward a unified opposition to the U.N. This does not mean that all conservatives oppose the U.N. for the same reasons. Some see the U.N. as a nascent world government waiting to shred our Constitution and national sovereignty. Others see it as an obstacle to an American-led international order. But in any event, increasing numbers of mainstream conservatives are arriving at the conclusion that the U.N., like the League of Nations, is not all that it is cracked up to be.

Truth be told, the U.N. is both inherently incapable of dealing with many crises and fundamentally at odds with the political vision of our Founding Fathers. It counts numerous tyrannical regimes among its members in good standing. In the General Assembly, the votes of dictatorships count for as much as the votes of free nations. In the Security Council, veto power is held not just by countries like Britain and the U.S. One permanent member, China, is a communist dictatorship while another, Russia, was one until a little more than a decade ago and retains many vestiges of repression.

Western Nations Are to Blame

The U.N.'s fabled concern for human rights has been selective to say the least. The body's conferences tend to blame Western nations for the word's ills and propose the redistribution of wealth as the solution. The two countries that are most frequently criticized in this debating society are the U.S. and Israel, despite the fact that the former is a significant source of funding. Some members actually see it is a potential counterweight to American world power. It was basically useless during the biggest struggle of its existence, the Cold War, and may prove to be equally so in the war on terrorism.

Of course, the U.N. may survive this test of its relevance. An America under economic strain may rely on its international relief agencies to play a large role in postwar Iraq. A failure on the part of coalition forces to find any significant stockpiles of prohibited weapons of mass destruction will be seen by many as a validation of the inspectors. Some U.N. critics may move on to other issues after the war is over, with no more interest in criticizing [UN secretary-general] Kofi Annan than they had in criticizing [French president] Jacques Chirac before the war debate.

Nevertheless, it is apparent that many people are now rethinking both the utility of international organizations like the U.N. and the vitality of the nation-state. In recent years, people have confidently asserted that the United Nations represents the future while the nation-state represents the past. So far, the conduct of the Iraq war cast considerable doubt upon these claims.

*"US eagerness to obtain a favorable UN
decision [on going to war with Iraq] belies
the Bush team charge that the UN risks
irrelevance."*

The U.S. War on Terrorism Has Not Diminished the Relevance of the United Nations

Terrell E. Arnold

According to Terrell E. Arnold in the following viewpoint, President George W. Bush's claim that the United Nations is irrelevant is wrong. The United Nations is the only global organization willing and able to deal with global problems such as AIDS, human rights violations, and terrorism, he argues. Arnold contends that only the United Nations can mobilize all nations to mount the serious and sustained attack necessary to end terrorism and other global problems. Terrell E. Arnold is a retired senior foreign service officer of the U.S. Department of State.

As you read, consider the following questions:

1. According to the author, why is President George W. Bush questioning the relevance and legitimacy of the United Nations?
2. In Arnold's opinion, what global issues give rise to the world's terrorists?
3. What does Arnold argue the United States should do instead of undermining the United Nations?

In the heat of debate to justify a war on Iraq,[1] top US leaders have attempted to make UN acceptance of the US position a test of the validity of the United Nations system. President [George W.] Bush did this at his ranch in Crawford, Texas last Saturday [in February 2003], and asserted again in a speech Wednesday that the United Nations had a last chance to prove its relevance by adopting a resolution the United States with British help will propose in a few days.

This week members of the Bush team have gone further by asserting that the UN will destroy its legitimacy by failing to back the US war plan. Like many of the throwaway lines Bush himself is fond of using, such as [Israeli prime minister] Ariel Sharon is "a man of peace", these comments are part of the in your face and personal style Bush and particularly his Secretary of Defense [Donald Rumsfeld] have adopted for putting down people who disagree with them.

Bush team members apparently are not willing to confront the real issue: whether a war on Iraq is either the necessary or the best way of disarming [Iraqi leader] Saddam [Hussein], or, more pointedly, whether disarming Saddam is even important at this time. Questioning the relevancy and the legitimacy of the UN is not only immature and impulsive, it is an underhanded and dangerous challenge to the only organization the world now has for dealing with a host of problems that neither the United States nor any other country can or should want to tackle alone. At the top of that list are AIDS, world hunger, human rights, failures and deficiencies in the nation state system, and the real war on terrorism.

Root Causes of Terrorism

Those problems cluster around the main global issues that gave rise to most if not all of the world's terrorists: Hunger, poverty, disease, social, political and economic injustice, political exclusion, and matters of cultural, ethnic or religious diversity. If not addressed, those issues will continue to generate new terrorists faster than they can be cut down in any

1. In 2003 the United States led a coalition to depose Iraqi leader Saddam Hussein. According to the Bush administration, Hussein was amassing weapons of mass destruction and aiding terrorists.

war on terrorism the United States can mount. That is simply because the present War on Terrorism is designed to capture, confine, kill or counter the existing terrorists, not to deal with the root causes of terrorism.

The US foreign assistance budget is neither large enough nor well-targeted enough to do much work on the global issues. With at least a third of that budget going to Israel and more than half going to Israel and Egypt together, the rest of the developing world receives very little. Meanwhile, as part of the bargaining around support for the war on Iraq, Israel is asking for $18 billion (to stay at home and fight its own battle) and Turkey is asking for and may get $30 billion (to support US war plans). Between them these two countries are asking for almost 6 times the entire US aid budget, more than the US trade deficit, to play their parts in the Iraq war.

Those war related expenditures and the de-facto bribes that may be paid to African or other members of the Security Council to get their votes on a new resolution are stark reminders that the US case for war with Iraq needs a great deal of work. Weaknesses in the case along with obvious signs of US desperation to get a favorable vote out of the UN have perverse effects for the US position: On the one hand, members of the Security Council and regional countries of importance to the US battle plan see plainly that the US can be had in the diplomatic bargaining. On the other hand, US eagerness to obtain a favorable UN decision belies the Bush team charge that the UN risks irrelevance or loss of legitimacy.

Only the UN Can Tackle Global Issues

In fact, the United Nations has the only forum where the United States can legitimate its plans, assuming they should be legitimated. During the Cold War, NATO [North Atlantic Treaty Organization] may have been a legitimating forum, but that no longer works. If the debate were properly focused by the Bush team, it would be about the legitimacy of the war, not about the standing of the UN. As shown in peace demonstrations in many countries last week, messengers from many parts of the world are saying the war is a poor idea. Killing the messengers or belittling them will not improve the plans. As the debate is being pursued, the UN is not standing in the way, it is serving in loco parentis for dealing with truculent and stubborn US posturing.

Several truths about the situation are obvious: The risks of terrorism cannot be greatly diminished without resolving the global issues. The real war on terrorism is not now being fought by the United States. War on Iraq will not do anything significant to diminish world terrorism. Whoever takes the lead in the war on terrorism must have global access. Only the UN has the standing needed to tackle the global issues. Only a serious and sustained attack by all nations on the global issues will assure any success in the war on terrorism. The outcome will never be perfect—the irrational element will always be there, and some protection against terrorism will always be necessary.

The United States on its best day cannot substitute for a detached international organization that is charged and

---

The UN Is Still Relevant

The world's view, with which the United States seems to agree, notwithstanding its policy of "assertive unilateralism," is that the UN is still relevant and should continue to exist.

The factors underlying this view, in broadest outline, are:

• *The "power bloc" system of international alliances that led to two world wars is no more a guarantor of peace today than it was in the past.* The fears expressed by Russia stemming from the expansion of NATO [North Atlantic Treaty Organization], and the disquiet over disarmament many in the West express over this move, seem ample indication of this problem.

• *The world is a vastly more complicated place now than it was at the end of World War II.* There are about 165 more countries in existence today than in 1945 when the UN was founded. Of these, 135 are UN members out of a total of 185 countries in the world. All of the new nations are poor and relatively weak. In a world that has become inextricably interdependent, nations require access to a common forum where their views can be heard and through which their interests can be protected. . . . The chances of war breaking out somewhere are extremely high. Thus, there is still a need for international peacekeeping interventions.

• *There are common issues such as disarmament, drug trafficking, and international crime which, due to their transnational charac-*

---

funded to do this work. But the United States with its wealth and technology can fuel the process. The risk is that, on the courses being taken by the Bush team, with only about 4% of the world's people, the United States will make itself irrelevant to managing the present conflict environment. Since [the September 11, 2001, terrorist attacks on the United States] US leadership has done an incredible job of blowing its opportunity to really attack world terrorism by too narrowly defining the problem, too exclusively defining the victims who matter, and too assiduously protecting the Israelis whose actions against the Palestinians are the current most potent generators of terrorism.

The Role of the UN Must Be Enhanced

Over the long haul, the roles and capabilities of the United Nations system must be enhanced and their funding must be

---

ter, individual governments cannot adequately cope alone. Moreover, there are problems such as refugee populations which, while impacting individual countries differently, require concerted international action for their resolution.

• *The UN, despite the controversy surrounding it (primarily in the United States), has a proven "track record."*

In the area of peacekeeping for example, it has undertaken forty-three missions (including seventeen still active today), negotiated 172 peaceful settlements that have ended regional conflicts, and enabled people in more than forty-five countries to participate in free and fair elections.

In the area of humanitarian and relief operations, its work in Africa, Asia, the Middle East, and Europe, caring for refugees and providing food, is well known.

In the unsung area of development assistance, it provides aid to more than 170 developing and "emerging" countries and territories that contain the bulk of the world's population. In collaboration with its affiliated Specialized Agencies, it has helped to make safe drinking water available to 1.3 billion people, halved child mortality rates, improved agricultural productivity, education, and health standards, and undertaken a myriad of other activities designed to help improve the lives of people.

Jerrold I. Berke, *American Diplomacy*, July 4, 1997. www.unc.edu.

---

markedly increased. Instead of an immature effort to undermine the UN, the United States should take the lead in assuring the UN has every tool it needs to be effective. Attacking the global issues with any hope of resolving them is a slow and patient process, even with adequate funding.

In moving to support the UN, the United States must stand for consistency and clarity on the most frightening aspect of the present and future threat of terrorism: The availability of weapons of mass destruction [WMDs] to nation states and potential leakage to terrorists. No one really quibbles with the effort to prevent additional countries from acquiring such weapons. But that outcome is not attainable in a world where the strong may have such weapons and the weak may not. There is no solution but to suppress them all. No one but the weapons owner will ever agree that he or she has any unique right to own such weapons. Their mere presence will generate that horrible fear, envy, or longing of the have nots that has led us where we are.

In the end, this problem can be managed only by detached leadership, and no nation state is capable of providing that. The four-tiered system that now exists cannot be sustained. That system consists of: (1) The pre-1967 members of the nuclear club who are in the nuclear Non Proliferation Treaty (NPT); (2) the Indians and the Pakistanis who are admitted proliferaters outside the NPT; (3) the Israelis who have weapons and are not admitted proliferaters but are outside the NPT and protected by the United States; and (4) everybody else who is not allowed to have such weapons. The obvious inconsistency of this system is part of the problem of dealing with Iraq, North Korea, or others such as Iran.

Another part of the problem is the availability of various weapons technologies and precursors from many developed countries for which no effective single export control or monitoring authority exists. The present honor system obviously works quite well to make trouble for us. That is amply shown by the case of Iraq where whatever capability exists derived from inputs of the United States, Germany, Russia and others, while Israel's weapons were made possible with French, US, British and other support.

Stopping Nuclear Proliferation

Some version of the International Atomic Energy Agency with teeth is likely to be the only long-term solution to proliferation problems. The UN is the only organization with any developed potential for overseeing that role. But the most intractable problem will be to persuade existing nuclear powers to shed their weapons.

The proliferation problems facing the UN, if it is properly given the mission, grow daily more complex. Given modern electronics, electromagnetic pulse weapons, modern explosives, delivery systems, and related technologies, the modern military force is a weapon of mass destruction without benefit of WMDs as such. Viewed realistically, recent civil wars and insurgencies in West Africa have demonstrated that concentrated numbers and reckless uses of small arms amount to weapons of mass destruction. US and British uses of U-238 or depleted uranium in the first Gulf War as a tank killer charge introduced a low grade nuclear weapon onto the modern battlefield, and the tens of thousands of Iraqi and American casualties of exposure to those devices made clear they are long term weapons of mass destruction. Those devices remind us that the ultimate weapon of mass destruction is, as it always has been, human intemperance.

In short, for the UN, the future proliferation problem is not just technical weapons of mass destruction, but the sheer mayhem that is possible in modern warfare. The immediate UN challenge is to prevent that mayhem from being visited upon Iraq.

Periodical Bibliography

The following articles have been selected to supplement the diverse views presented in this chapter.

Kofi A. Annan	"Fighting Terrorism on a Global Front," *New York Times*, September 21, 2001.
Christian Science Monitor	"A Not-So-Irrelevant UN," May 21, 2003. www.csmonitor.com.
Onkar Ghate	"America Is Not Winning the War," *Media Link*, August 26, 2002. www.aynrand.org.
Victor Davis Hanson	"War Will Be War," *National Review*, May 6, 2002.
Elan Journo and Yaron Brook	"The Timid War on Terror," *Media Link*, September 4, 2003. www.aynrand.org.
Matthew Levinger	"U.S. Invasion of Iraq Would Play into Bin Laden's Hands," *Seattle Post-Intelligencer*, October 4, 2002. http://seattlepi.nwsource.com.
John T. Middleton	"World Is Now a Safer Place," *Press-Republican*, June 26, 2003. www.pressrepublican.com.
Don Monkerud	"Are We Any Safer Now?" *Santa Cruz Sentinel*, December 7, 2003. www.santacruzsentinel.com.
Raphael Perl	"Terrorism and National Security: Trends and Issues," *CRS Issue Brief for Congress*, May 12, 2003.
John B. Quigley	"War on Terrorism Won't Be Won Unless Policy Is Changed to Counter Resentment," *Columbus Dispatch*, December 17, 2003. www.dispatch.com.
Karina Rollins	"No Compromises: Why We're Going to Lose the War on Terror . . . and How We Could Win," *American Enterprise*, January/February 2003.
Brett D. Schaffer	"UN Treaties and Conferences Will Not Stop Terrorism," *Heritage Foundation Backgrounder*, January 17, 2002. www.heritage.org.
Jack Spencer and Ha Nguyen	"Is U.S. Safer Since September 11 Attacks?" *Heritage Foundation Policy Research and Analysis*, September 15, 2003. www.heritage.org.
Shaun Waterman	"Iraq War May Have Made Terror Threat Worse," *United Press International*, July 9, 2003. www.upi.com.
Sam Webb	"War on Terror Makes the World More Dangerous," *People's Weekly World*, January 19, 2002. www.pww.org.

For Further Discussion

Chapter 1

1. Dr. Leonard Peikoff argues that the United States has the right to defend itself against terrorism by going to war against those nations that support terrorism. Editors of the British *Independent/ UK* insist that the war on terrorism is unsuccessful and has exacerbated war and terror worldwide. Which author is more persuasive? Why?

2. According to Michael T. Klare, the U.S. war against terrorism provides a convenient rationale for continued military involvement in oil-producing countries such as Iraq. However, Peter Ferrara insists that the United States does not have to start a war that costs billions of dollars and countless American lives when it can buy all the oil it needs directly from Iraq or from worldwide oil brokers. Which viewpoint do you think is more convincing? Please explain your answer.

3. Jim Lobe argues that the September 11, 2001, terrorist attacks on the United States provided neoconservatives with the excuse they needed to launch a war against Iraq. He maintains that the purpose of the war is not to fight terrorism but to put the United States on a road to global dominance. President George W. Bush, however, insists that the war in Iraq is a war to fight terrorism and bring democracy to the Iraqi people and other nations throughout the world. In your opinion, which author makes the stronger argument? Explain.

4. Joseph Cirincione argues that the Iraq war was unnecessary and unjustified. He maintains that Iraqi leader Saddam Hussein has no links to al Qaeda. However, Dan Darling insists that Iraq presented an imminent threat to the United States because it was in collusion with al Qaeda terrorists. Which argument is more convincing? Why?

Chapter 2

1. Kelly Patricia O'Meara insists that the USA PATRIOT Act sacrifices civil liberties for national security and provides little help in the war on terrorism. Kate O'Beirne, however, argues that the act fights terrorism without threatening civil liberties. Is it acceptable to sacrifice some civil liberties for increased security? Explain.

2. Peter G. Simonson argues that any benefits to the war on terrorism that may come from racial profiling are outweighed by the harm it does to race relations and civil liberties. However,

according to Roger Clegg, racial profiling to prevent terrorism is not a violation of civil liberties. Which viewpoint is more convincing? Why?

3. Anita Ramasastry maintains that "preventive detention" of immigrants in the hope that future terrorist attacks will be stopped is a violation of civil liberties. Bradford A. Berenson and Richard Klingler argue that immigrant detention is legal and so limited in scope that it does not threaten civil liberties. Discuss the evidence both authors offer to support their arguments. Which uses evidence most convincingly?

Chapter 3

1. Tom Ridge claims that the Department of Homeland Security will make Americans safer because it consolidates many government departments and gives responsibility for the nation's safety to one agency. Ron Paul, however, argues that the Department of Homeland Security will create confusion and inefficiencies, and that the consolidation of so much power in one federal department is a threat to Americans' liberty. In your opinion, will reorganization of the federal government make America safer? Explain your answer, citing from the viewpoints.

2. John Perazzo claims that illegal immigration presents a threat to the United States. Illegal aliens, he insists, have taken part in almost every major attack on the United States perpetrated by Islamic terrorists. Illegal immigrants, particularly refugees, are not a terrorist threat, Donald Kerwin argues. He points out that most terrorists enter the United States using legal visas. In your opinion, which viewpoint is more persuasive? Why?

3. Kathleen Parker argues that arming airline pilots is the best way to prevent airplane hijackings. George Will, however, contends that the best way pilots can keep their passengers safe is to land their planes safely—something they cannot do if they are busy fighting terrorists. In your opinion, would arming pilots increase or reduce passenger safety? Defend your answer using quotes from the viewpoints.

4. John D. Woodward Jr. argues that face recognition technology provides accurate, instantaneous identification of individuals and is therefore a valuable tool in the fight against terrorism. Philip E. Agre insists that face recognition technology provides too many false positive matches to be considered useful in identifying terrorists. In your opinion, which argument is more persuasive? Why?

Chapter 4

1. Colin L. Powell points to a drop in the number of terrorist attacks worldwide from 2001 to 2002 to argue that the U.S. war on terrorism is causing a decrease in terrorist acts worldwide. Georgie Anne Geyer insists that the war in the Middle East is breeding anger and resentment, which will lead to an increase in terrorist activity. Which argument is stronger? Explain, citing from the viewpoints.

2. Andrew Bernstein argues that the U.S. war on terrorism is undermining the Israeli battle against terrorism. In contrast, the editors of *Impact* maintain that Israel should receive uncompromising encouragement and support from the United States in its fight against terrorism. In your opinion, who makes the more persuasive argument? Why?

3. Only the United Nations has the power and presence necessary to mobilize all nations to mount the sustained attacked required to end terrorism, Terrell E. Arnold argues. In contrast, W. James Antle III maintains that the United Nations' refusal to abide by its own resolutions and support the U.S. position advocating the use of force against regimes that support terrorists renders the organization irrelevant in today's world. Given what each author has to say about the United Nations' role in the world today, do you think the organization is still relevant? Explain your answer.

Organizations to Contact

The editors have compiled the following list of organizations concerned with the issues debated in this book. The descriptions are derived from materials provided by the organizations. All have publications or information available for interested readers. The list was compiled on the date of publication of the present volume; the information provided here may change. Be aware that many organizations take several weeks or longer to respond to inquiries, so allow as much time as possible.

American Civil Liberties Union (ACLU)
125 Broad St., 18th Floor, New York, NY 10004-2400
(212) 549-2500
e-mail: aclu@aclu.org • Web site: www.aclu.org

The American Civil Liberties Union is a national organization that works to defend Americans' civil rights guaranteed by the U.S. Constitution, arguing that measures to protect national security should not compromise fundamental civil liberties. It publishes and distributes policy statements, pamphlets, and press releases with titles such as "In Defense of Freedom in a Time of Crisis" and "National ID Cards: 5 Reasons Why They Should Be Rejected."

Anti-Defamation League (ADL)
823 United Nations Plaza, New York, NY 10017
(212) 885-7700 • fax: (212) 867-0779
Web site: www.adl.org

The Anti-Defamation League is a human relations organization dedicated to combating all forms of prejudice and bigotry. The league has placed a spotlight on terrorism and on the dangers posed for extremism. Its Web site records reactions to the September 11, 2001, terrorist incidents by both extremist and mainstream organizations, provides background information on Osama bin Laden, and furnishes other materials on terrorism and the Middle East. The ADL also maintains a bimonthly online newsletter, *Frontline*.

Ayn Rand Institute (ARI)
2121 Alton Parkway, Suite 250, Irvine, CA 92606-4926
(949) 222-6550 • fax: (949) 222-6558
e-mail: mail@aynrand.org • Web site: www.aynrand.org

The Ayn Rand Institute helps establish a culture of reason by spreading Ayn Rand's philosophy of objectivism. Objectivism's viewpoint—reason not mysticism, the individual not the collective, free markets and free minds not government controls—offers a unique perspective on events and issues including the war on terrorism. The September 2002 issue of ARI's monthly newsletter *Impact* is devoted to "America at War." In addition, ARI publishes online at www.medialink.org, where articles presenting the rational ideas to win the war against Islamic terrorism and the states that support it can be found.

The Brookings Institution
1775 Massachusetts Ave. NW, Washington, DC 20036
(202) 797-6000 • fax: (202) 797-6004
e-mail: brookinfo@brook.edu • Web site: www.brookings.org

The institution, founded in 1927, is a think tank that conducts research and education in foreign policy, economics, government, and the social sciences. In 2001 it began America's Response to Terrorism, a project that provides briefings and analysis to the public and which is featured on the center's Web site. Other publications include the quarterly *Brookings Review*, periodic *Policy Briefs*, and books including *Terrorism and U.S. Foreign Policy*.

CATO Institute
1000 Massachusetts Ave. NW, Washington, DC 20001-5403
(202) 842-0200 • fax: (202) 842-3490
e-mail: cato@cato.org • Web site: www.cato.org

The institute is a nonpartisan public policy research foundation dedicated to limiting the role of government and protecting individual liberties. It publishes the quarterly magazine *Regulation*, the bimonthly *Cato Policy Report*, and numerous policy papers and articles. Works on terrorism include "Does U.S. Intervention Overseas Breed Terrorism?" and "Military Tribunals No Answer."

Center for Contemporary Conflict (CCC) at the Naval Postgraduate School
1 University Circle, Monterey, CA 93943
(831) 656-2441
e-mail: daschlei@nps.navy.mil • Web site: www.ccc.nps.navy.mil

The Center for Contemporary Conflict is the research institute of the Naval Postgraduate School's Department of National Security Affairs. The CCC analyzes current and emerging threats to U.S. national security. Research topics include asymmetric conflicts such as terrorism and counterterrorism, weapons of mass destruction, regional instability such as the Israeli-Palestinian conflict, and strategic military policy. The CCC publishes *Strategic Insight*, a monthly journal that offers timely, concise assessments of U.S. and international security issues including terrorism. It is available on-line at the organization's Web site.

Center for Defense Information
1779 Massachusetts Ave. NW, Suite 615, Washington, DC 20036
(202) 332-0600 • fax: (202) 462-4559
e-mail: info@cdi.org • Web site: www.cdi.org

The Center for Defense Information is a nonpartisan, nonprofit organization that researches all aspects of global security. It seeks to educate the public and policy makers about issues such as weapons systems, security policy, and defense budgeting. It publishes the monthly publication *Defense Monitor*, the issue brief "National Missile Defense: What Does It All Mean?" and the studies "Homeland Security: A Competitive Strategies Approach" and "Reforging the Sword."

Center for Immigration Studies
1522 K St. NW, Suite 820, Washington, DC 20005-1202
(202) 466-8185 • fax: (202) 466-8076
e-mail: center@cis.org • Web site: www.cis.org

The Center for Immigration Studies is the nation's only think tank dedicated to research and analysis of the economic, social, and demographic impacts of immigration on the United States. An independent, nonpartisan, nonprofit research organization founded in 1985, the center aims to expand public support for an immigration policy that is both proimmigrant and low-immigration. Among its publications are the backgrounders "The USA PATRIOT Act of 2001: A Summary of the Anti-Terrorism Law's Immigration-Related Provisions" and "America's Identity Crisis: Document Fraud Is Pervasive and Pernicious."

Center for Strategic and International Studies (CSIS)
1800 K St. NW, Suite 400, Washington, DC 20006
(202) 887-0200 • fax: (202) 775-3199
Web site: www.csis.org

The center works to provide world leaders with strategic insights and policy options on current and emerging global issues. It publishes books including *To Prevail: An American Strategy for the Campaign Against Terrorism*, the *Washington Quarterly*, a journal on political, economic, and security issues, and other publications including reports that can be downloaded from its Web site.

Central Intelligence Agency (CIA)

Office of Public Affairs, Washington, DC 20505
(703) 482-0623 • fax: (703) 482-1739
Web site: www.cia.gov

President Harry S. Truman created the CIA in 1947 with the signing of the National Security Act (NSA). The NSA charged the director of central intelligence (DCI) with coordinating the nation's intelligence activities and correlating, evaluating, and disseminating intelligence that affects national security. The CIA is an independent agency, responsible to the president through the DCI, and accountable to the American people through the Intelligence Oversight Committee of the U.S. Congress. Publications, including *Factbook on Intelligence*, are available on its Web site.

Council on American-Islamic Relations (CAIR)

453 New Jersey Ave. SE, Washington, DC 20003
(202) 488-8787 • fax: (202) 488-0833
e-mail: cair@cair-net.org • Web site: www.cair-net.org

CAIR is a nonprofit membership organization that presents an Islamic perspective on public policy issues and challenges the misrepresentation of Islam and Muslims. It publishes the quarterly newsletter *Faith in Action* and other various publications on Muslims in the United States. Its Web site includes statements condemning both the September 11 attacks and discrimination against Muslims.

Department of Homeland Security (DHS)

Washington, DC 20528
Web site: www.dhs.gov

The Department of Homeland Security was created in direct response to the terrorist attacks of September 11, 2001. It was the largest reshaping of the federal government since 1949. With this change, many formerly disparate offices became united in a mission to prevent terrorist attacks on American soil, reduce the country's vulnerability to terrorism, and effectively respond to attacks that did occur. The Department of Homeland Security took branches formerly of the Departments of Treasury, Justice, Agriculture, Energy, Commerce, Transportation, and Defense under its extensive wing. Services from the Coast Guard to Customs are now linked under the same umbrella, all with the singular mission of protecting the United States from attack. Among other information, the DHS Web site offers access to the Homeland Security Advisory System, a color-coded chart that indicates current terrorist threat levels.

Federal Aviation Administration (FAA)

800 Independence Ave. SW, Washington, DC 20591
(800) 322-7873 • fax: (202) 267-3484
Web site: www.faa.gov

The Federal Aviation Administration is the component of the U.S. Department of Transportation whose primary responsibility is the safety of civil aviation. The FAA's major functions include regulating civil aviation to promote safety and fulfill the requirements of national defense. Among its publications are *Technology Against Terrorism*, *Air Piracy*, *Airport Security, and International Terrorism: Winning the War Against Hijackers*, and *Security Tips for Air Travelers*.

Federal Bureau of Investigation (FBI)

935 Pennsylvania Ave. NW, Room 7972, Washington, DC 20535
(202) 324-3000
Web site: www.fbi.gov

The FBI, the principle investigative arm of the U.S. Department of Justice, evolved from an unnamed force of special agents formed on July 26, 1909. It has the authority and responsibility to investigate specific crimes assigned to it. The FBI also is authorized to provide other law enforcement agencies with cooperative services, such as fingerprint identification, laboratory examinations, and police training. The mission of the FBI is to uphold the law through the investigation of violations of federal criminal law; to protect the United States from foreign intelligence and terrorist activities; to provide leadership and law enforcement assistance to federal, state, local, and international agencies; and to perform these responsibilities in a manner that is responsive to the needs of the public and is faithful to the Constitution of the United States. Press releases, congressional statements, and major speeches on issues concerning the FBI are available on the agency's Web site.

Institute for Policy Studies (IPS)

733 15th St. NW, Suite 1020, Washington, DC 20005
(202) 234-9382 • fax (202) 387-7915
Web site: www.ips-dc.org

The Institute for Policy Studies is a progressive think tank that works to develop societies built around the values of justice and nonviolence. It publishes reports including *Global Perspectives: A Media Guide to Foreign Policy Experts*. Numerous articles and interviews on September 11 and terrorism are available on its Web site.

International Policy Institute of Counter-Terrorism (ICT)
PO Box 167, Herzlia 46150, Israel
972-9-9527277 • fax: 972-9-9513073
e-mail: mail@ict.org.il • Web site: www.ict.org.il

ICT is a research institute dedicated to developing public policy solutions to international terrorism. The ICT Web site is a comprehensive resource on terrorism and counterterrorism, featuring an extensive database and terrorist attacks and organizations, including al Qaeda.

Islamic Supreme Council of America (ISCA)
1400 16th St. NW, Room B112, Washington, DC 20036
(202) 939-3400 • fax: (202) 939-3410
e-mail: staff@islamicsupremecouncil.org
Web site: www.islamicsupremecouncil.org

The ISCA is a nongovernmental religious organization that promotes Islam in America both by providing practical solutions to American Muslims in integrating Islamic teachings with American culture and by teaching non-Muslims that Islam is a religion of moderation, peace, and tolerance. It strongly condemns Islamic extremists and all forms of terrorism. Its Web site includes statements, commentaries, and reports on terrorism, including *Osama bin Laden: A Legend Gone Wrong* and *Jihad: A Misunderstood Concept from Islam*.

National Security Agency
9800 Savage Rd., Ft. Meade, MD 20755-6248
(301) 688-6524
Web site: www.nsa.gov

The National Security Agency coordinates, directs, and performs activities, such as designing cipher systems, which protect American information systems and produce foreign intelligence information. It is the largest employer of mathematicians in the United States and hires the nation's best codemakers and codebreakers. Speeches, briefings, and reports are available at the Web site.

U.S. Department of State, Counterterrorism Office
Office of Public Affairs, Room 2507
2201 C St. NW, Washington, DC 20520
(202) 647-4000
e-mail: secretary@state.gov • Web site: www.state.gov/s/ct

The office works to develop and implement American counterterrorism strategy and to improve cooperation with foreign governments. Articles and speeches by government officials are available at its Web site.

Bibliography of Books

Nafeez Mosaddeq Ahmed	*Behind the War on Terror: Western Secret Strategy and the Struggle for Iraq.* Philadelphia: New Society, 2003.
Nafeez Mosaddeq Ahmed and John Leonard	*The War on Freedom: How and Why America Was Attacked September 11, 2001.* Joshua Tree, CA: Tree of Life, 2002.
William J. Bennett	*Why We Fight: Moral Clarity and the War on Terrorism.* Washington, DC: Regnery, 2003.
Steven Brill	*After: How America Confronted the September 11 Era.* New York: Simon & Schuster, 2003.
James Brovard	*Terrorism and Tyranny: Trampling Freedom, Justice and Peace to Rid the World of Evil.* New York: Palgrave Macmillan, 2003.
Cynthia Brown, ed.	*Lost Liberties: Ashcroft and the Assault on Personal Freedom.* New York: New Press, 2003.
George W. Bush, Peggy Noonan, and Jay Nordlinger	*We Will Prevail: President George W. Bush on War, Terrorism, and Freedom.* New York: Continuum, 2003.
Michel Chossudovsky	*War and Globalisation: The Truth Behind September 11.* Oakland, CA: Global Outlook, 2002.
Wesley K. Clark	*Winning Modern Wars: Iraq, Terrorism and the American Empire.* New York: PublicAffairs, 2003.
Jane Corbin	*Al-Qaeda: In Search of the Terror Network That Threatens the World.* New York: Thunder's Mouth Press, 2002.
Ann Coulter	*Treason: Liberal Treachery from the Cold War to the War on Terrorism.* New York: Crown Forum, 2003.
Jean Bethke Elshtain	*Just War Against Terror: The Burden of American Power in a Violent World.* New York: Basic Books, 2003.
David Frum and Richard Perle	*An End to Evil: How to Win the War on Terror.* New York: Random House, 2003.
Victor Hanson	*An Autumn of War: What America Learned from September 11 and the War on Terrorism.* New York: Anchor Books/Doubleday, 2002.
Stephen Hess and Marvil Kalb, eds.	*The Media and the War on Terrorism.* Washington, DC: Brookings Institution, 2003.
Walter Laqueur	*No End to War: Terrorism in the Twenty-first Century.* New York: Continuum, 2003.

Walter Laqueur and Barry Rubin, eds.	*The Arab-Israeli Reader: A Documentary History of the Middle East Conflict.* New York: Penguin USA, 2001.
Richard C. Leone and Greg Anrig Jr., eds.	*The War on Our Freedoms: Civil Liberties in an Age of Terrorism.* New York: PublicAffairs, 2003.
Rahul Mahajan	*Full Spectrum Dominance: U.S. Power in Iraq and Beyond.* New York: Seven Stories Press, 2003.
Bill Maher	*When You Ride Alone You Ride with Bin Laden: What the Government Should Be Telling Us to Help Fight the War on Terrorism.* Portland, OR: New Millennium Press, 2003.
Julianne Malveaux and Reginna A. Green, eds.	*The Paradox of Loyalty: An African American Response to the War on Terrorism.* Chicago: Third World Press, 2002.
T.C. Mann	*The War on Terror (for the Common Man).* Philadelphia: Xlibris, 2003.
Robin Moore	*The Hunt for Bin Laden.* New York: Random House, 2003.
Laurie Mylroie	*Bush vs. the Beltway: How the CIA and the State Department Tried to Stop the War on Terror.* New York: Regan Books, 2003.
Ralph Peters	*Beyond Baghdad: Postmodern War and Peace.* Mechanicsburg, PA: Stackpole Books, 2003.
William Rivers Pitt	*The Greatest Sedition Is Silence: Four Fears in America.* London: Pluto Press, 2003.
Marcus Ranum	*The Myth of Homeland Security.* Hoboken, NJ: John Wiley and Sons, 2003.
Daniel Ratner and Mark Ratner	*Nanotechnology and Homeland Security: New Weapons for New Wars.* Saddle River, NJ: Prentice Hall/PTR, 2003.
Bruce Schneier	*Beyond Fear: Thinking Sensibly About Security in an Uncertain World.* New York: Copernicus, 2003.
Paul Sperry	*Crude Politics: How Bush's Oil Cronies Hijacked the War on Terrorism.* Nashville: WND Books, 2003.
Gore Vidal	*Dreaming War: Blood for Oil and the Cheney-Bush Junto.* New York: Thunder's Mouth Press, 2002.
Eliot Weinberger	*9/12: New York After.* Chicago: Prickly Paradigm, 2003.
Bob Woodward	*Bush at War.* New York: Simon & Schuster, 2002.

Index